脱文法

100トピック
実践英語
トレーニング

Intuitive Grammar English
Training: 100 Topics

中山誠一
Jacob Schnickel
Juergen Bulach
山内博之

ひつじ書房

◆ この本の使い方 ◆

　本書は、英文法が苦手、英語が苦手な方でも確実に英語の話す力と聞く力がつけられるテキストです。本書1冊をマスターすれば、ほぼどんな場面でも英語で困ることはありません。本書には次の3つの特徴があります。

　1つめは、扱っているトピックの広さです。社会生活で遭遇するあらゆる話題を100種類にまとめてあります。これだけの英語をマスターすれば、日常生活のみでなく、ビジネスや国際会議などにも対応できます。

　2つめは、言語運用能力を規定しているCEFRという国際基準に準拠していることです。本書は、CEFRのB1レベルを目指して作成されています。B1レベルの英語力があれば、どんな場面でもほとんど困ることはありません。

　3つめは、「瞬間トランスレーション（瞬トラ）」という本書独自の学習法を採り入れていることです。「瞬トラ」を1日に何度も繰り返すことによって、英文法の知識がなくても英語が話せるようになります。

　これらの特徴を合わせた本書があれば、英語はもう怖くありません。

1．質問しよう

　会話は「質問すること」とその質問に「応答すること」から成り立っています。つまり、「質問する能力」と「応答する能力」は車の両輪のような関係で、どちらが欠けても会話は成り立ちません。そこで、このセクションでは、まず「質問する能力」を身につけます。そのトピックのターゲットとなる質問が難易度順に3つ並んでいます。A1は一言で答えられる質問、A2は一文で答えられる質問、B1は段落で答える質問です。まず、これらの質問の内容を確認したら、3つの質問文を覚えてしまいましょう。本書には、質問は合計で600あります。これだけの質問を覚えれば、話題には困りません。

2．答えよう

　このセクションには、「1．質問しよう」で示された質問に対する回答例が示されています。答えられない質問があれば、①回答例をよく読んで意味を理解し、②音声を聞いて、最初はパラレル・リーディング、③次にシャドーイングをしましょう。パラレル・リーディングとは、音

声を聞きながら、その音声に遅れないようにテキストを音読していく練習法です。シャドーイングとは、録音された音声を聞きながら、テキストを見ずに、聞こえたことをほぼ同時に言っていく練習法です。電車の中などでは、声を出さずに口を動かすだけでもかまいません。通学や通勤の時に行えば、時間の有効活用にもなります。B1 の回答は A1 や A2 の質問の回答より長いので、パラレル・リーディングやシャドーイングが難しければ、次の「3．練習しよう」に移りましょう。

3．練習しよう

日本語を英語に変換するためには、2つの能力が必要です。1つは日本語を単語レベルで英語に変換する能力で、もう1つは英単語を英語の語順に変換する能力です。どちらが欠けても英語は話せません。そこで、このセクションでは、これら2つの能力を養成するために「瞬トラ」を行います。

①単語ごとに英訳しよう

日本語を単語レベルで英語に変換する能力を育成します。B1 の質問に対する模範回答が1文ずつ示され、各英文の上に日本語が付記されています。英文を赤い下敷きで隠して、上の日本語を順に英語で言ってみてください。下の英文が自然に口から出てくることがわかると思います。最初はゆっくり、慣れてきたらどんどん速く言えるように練習してください。ある程度速く言えるようになったら、次に進みます。

②「／」ごとに英訳しよう

日本語をフレーズごとに英語に変換する能力を育成します。今度は単語ごとではなく、「／」ごとに一気に英語で言ってみましょう。最初はゆっくりでかまいません。慣れてきたらどんどん速く言えるように練習してください。速く言えるようになったら、もう1度音声を聞き、シャドーイングしてみてください。シャドーイングが完全にできたら、「2．答えよう」に戻って、下敷きで英文を隠し、日本語を見ながら、英文を一気に言う練習をしてみてください。それができたら、「4．覚えよう」に移り、回答全体を言う練習をします。最初は戸惑うかもしれませんが、10 トピックほどやってみてください。自分の言いたいことが、自然に英語の語順になって出てくるようになると思います。この方法なら、文法の知識がなくても、自然に英文を作ることができます。

4．覚えよう

最後の仕上げとして、B1の質問に対して何も見ずに回答全体を言う練習をします。単語やフレーズを換えてオリジナルの回答を作ってもよいでしょう。

5．話してみよう

各トピックの最後には練習問題があります。自信のある方はぜひチャレンジしてください。「5．話してみよう」は後回しにし、最後にまとめて復習や力試しとして使ってもかまいません。

「瞬間トランスレーション（瞬トラ）」について

「瞬間トランスレーション（瞬トラ）」は、本書が提案する、日本語母語話者のための英語トレーニング法です。次の表は、シャドーイング、パラレル・リーディング、瞬間トランスレーションの違いを一覧にして示したものです。

トレーニング名	インプット	アウトプット
シャドーイング	音（英語）	音（英語）
パラレル・リーディング	音・文字（英語）	音（英語）
瞬間トランスレーション	意味（日本語）	音（英語）

シャドーイングは、耳から入った英語の音を、瞬時にそのまま口から出すトレーニングです。つまり、耳から入るインプットが「英語の音」で、口から出るアウトプットも「英語の音」です。シャドーイングを行うと、聞き取り能力が向上し、口が回るようになります。口が回るようになるというのは、日本語にはない英語の音がスムーズに口から出るようになるということです。

パラレル・リーディングは、英語の音を聞きながら、同時に英語の文字も見て、耳から入る音声と同じ速度で口から英語を出していくトレーニングです。英語の音だけでなく、文字もインプットとして入ってくるので、シャドーイングよりも負荷が軽く、特に、英語を読むことに慣れている日本人にとっては、とっつきやすいトレーニングです。期待できる効果は、シャドーイングとほぼ同じですが、シャドーイングよりも負荷が軽いので、シャドーイングの前に行うのに適したトレーニングです。

シャドーイングとパラレル・リーディングを行うと、耳から入ってくる英語のインプットを処理する能力が向上するため、聞き取り能力が向上します。しかし、話す能力はあまり向上しません。そこで、本書が提案するのが「瞬間トランスレーション（瞬トラ）」です。入ってくるインプットを瞬間的に処理するという点は、シャドーイング、パラレル・リーディングと同じですが、瞬トラのインプットは、英語ではなく、日本語です。日本語母語話者であれば、日本語の意味は容易に理解できるので、それを瞬間的に英語に翻訳していきます。その際、インプットとして入ってくる日本語は、文ではなく、単語なので、並んでいる日本語の単語を逐語訳的に英語に変えていくだけで、英語の文が口から出ていくようになっています。つまり、文法を考えて文を組み立てるというプロセスは必要がないということです。瞬トラを使って、単語から単語、フレーズからフレーズ、そして文から文へと日本語を英語に変換する練習をすることにより、英語の発話力を着実に身につけることができます。

本書で学習すれば、絶対に英語が聞けるように、話せるようになります。最後まで諦めずに頑張ってください。

本書のホームページでこの本の使い方を紹介しています。
『脱文法　100トピック実践英語トレーニング』ウェブサイト
https://www.hituzi.co.jp/hituzibooks/ISBN978-4-89476-858-1.htm

◆この本で扱う話題(トピック)◆

　本書における話題設定の考え方は、山内博之編(2013)『実践日本語教育スタンダード』(ひつじ書房)に依拠しており、その内容は以下のとおりです。

言語活動	領域	分野	話題
サバイバル	生活	文化	「食」など10話題
		人生・生活	「町」など16話題
		人間関係	「家族」など8話題
		学校・勉強	「学校(小中高)」など6話題
ポストサバイバル	人文	芸術・趣味	「音楽」など13話題
		宗教・祭り	「宗教」など2話題
		歴史	「歴史」の1話題
	社会	メディア	「メディア」など2話題
		通信・コンピュータ	「通信」など2話題
		経済・消費	「買い物・家計」など8話題
		産業	「工業一般」など8話題
		社会	「事件・事故」など4話題
		政治	「政治」など7話題
	自然	ヒト・生き物	「人体」など5話題
		自然	「気象」など5話題
		サイエンス	「算数・数学」など3話題

　言語活動には、日常生活に不可欠な「サバイバル」の言語活動と、日常生活には必ずしも必要でない「ポストサバイバル」の言語活動があります。「サバイバル」の言語活動は「生活」という話題の領域によって支えられ、「ポストサバイバル」の言語活動は「人文」「社会」「自然」という話題の領域によって支えられています。また、これら4つの領域の下位には「文化」「人生・生活」「人間関係」など16の分野があり、そのそれぞれの中に「食」「町」などの個々の話題があります。『実践日本語教育スタンダード』では、話題の総数がちょうど100となっています。本書ではそのすべてを教材化し、順に配列しました。

◆ この本で扱う CEFR のレベル ◆

　CEFR には、能力の低い方から順に A1、A2、B1、B2、C1、C2 という６つのレベルがあります。下の表は、この本が扱う能力に最も近い「長く一人で話す：経験談」というカテゴリーの能力記述文です。この本の目標は、以下の表の B1 の言語活動ができるようになることです。

　日本人英語学習者の８割が A1、A2 レベルであるとも言われていますが、この本で徹底的に練習すれば、必ず B1 になれます。B1 になれば、日常生活ではあまり困らなくなりますし、英語を使って仕事をすることも可能になります。みなさん、B1 を目指して頑張ってください！！

B1	自分の関心事で、馴染みのあるさまざまな話題について、簡単に述べることができる。／比較的流暢に、簡単な語りができ、事柄を直線的に並べて述べることができる。／自分の感情や反応を描写しながら、経験を詳細に述べることができる。／予測不能の出来事（例えば事故など）を、順序だてて詳細に述べることができる。／本や映画の筋を順序だてて話し、それに対する自分の考えを述べることができる。／夢や希望、野心を述べることができる。／現実や想像上の出来事を述べることができる。／物語を順序だてて語ることができる。
A2	事柄を列挙して簡単に述べたり、物語ることができる。／自分の周りの環境、例えば、人や場所、仕事、学習経験などの日常を述べることができる。／出来事や活動の要点を短く述べることができる。／計画、準備、習慣、日々の仕事、過去の活動や個人の経験を述べることができる。／事物や所有物を比較し、簡単な言語を用いて短く述べることができる。／好きか嫌いかを述べることができる。
	家族、住居環境、学歴、現在やごく最近までしていた仕事を述べることができる。／簡単な言葉で人や場所、所有物を述べることができる。
A1	自分について、自分が何をしているか、自分が住んでいる場所を、述べることができる。

＊吉島茂・大橋理枝他 (訳・編) (2004)『外国語教育Ⅱ―外国語の学習、教授、評価のためのヨーロッパ共通参照枠―』（朝日出版社）より引用。

◆ 英語習得のコツ ◆

　英語習得のためには「日々の鍛錬」と「道場通い」が必要で、そのどちらが欠けても習得が困難になります。「道場通い」とは、英語を話す機会を定期的に持ち、コンスタントに英語を使い続けることです。英語の授業を履修すること、英会話サークルに入ること、英会話学校に通うことなどが、それに当たります。定期的に英語を使用し、自分の力を試すことが重要です。

　しかし、道場に通っているだけでは、絶対に英語は上達しません。だから、英語の授業をとっているからといって、また、英会話学校に通い始めたからといって、決して安心しないでください。それだけでは、絶対に英語は上達しません。

　英語上達の原動力となるものが「日々の鍛錬」です。具体的には、毎日、このテキストで、パラレル・リーディング、シャドーイング、瞬間トランスレーションに励んでください。パラレル・リーディングとシャドーイングで、耳がよくなり、口が回るようになります。そして、瞬間トランスレーションによって、自力で英語の長文が発話できるようになります。

　このようなトレーニングを毎日行うこと、つまり、「日々の鍛錬」こそが、英語能力を向上させるための主要な方法なのですが、道場に通わずに鍛錬を続けることは、現実的にはなかなか難しいです。何のために日々鍛錬するのか、その意味を見失いやすく、モチベーションを保つことが困難になります。人間、なかなかそこまで強くなれるものではありません。それに、そもそも、言語とは使うために存在するものであり、「実際に使うからこそ習得のために努力する」というのが、英語学習に対するごく自然な態度です。

　この本を使って日々鍛錬し、かつ定期的に英語を話す機会を持って、英語使用を楽しみつつ力試しをする、それが英語習得のコツです。「日々の鍛錬」と「道場通い」、この２つを継続すれば、英語は必ず習得できます。

目次

この本の使い方	iii
この本で扱う話題（トピック）	vii
この本で扱うCEFRのレベル	viii
英語習得のコツ	ix
音声データダウンロードについて	xv

[1] Culture／文化

1.	Clothing／衣	2
2.	Food／食	5
3.	Alcohol／酒	8
4.	Travel／旅行	11
5.	Sports／スポーツ	14
6.	Housing／住	17
7.	Languages／言葉	20
8.	Literature & Publications／文芸・出版	23
9.	Seasons & Events／季節・行事	26
10.	Culture in General／文化一般	29

[2] Life／人生・生活

11.	City Life／町	32
12.	Hometown／ふるさと	35
13.	Transportation／交通	38
14.	Daily Life／日常生活	41
15.	Home Electronics／家電・機械	44
16.	Housework／家事	47
17.	Parties／パーティー	50
18.	Moving／引越し	53

19.	Procedures／手続き	56
20.	Love／恋愛	59
21.	Marriage／結婚	62
22.	Childbirth & Childcare／出産・育児	65
23.	Memories／思い出	68
24.	Dreams & Goals／夢・目標	71
25.	Worries／悩み	74
26.	Death／死	77

[3] Human Relations／人間関係

27.	Family／家族	80
28.	Friendship／友達	83
29.	Personality／性格	86
30.	Feelings／感情	89
31.	Appearance／容姿	92
32.	Personal Relationships／人づきあい	95
33.	Disagreements & Arguments／喧嘩・トラブル	98
34.	Customs & Manners／マナー・習慣	101

[4] School & Study／学校・勉強

35.	Schools／学校（小・中・高等学校）	104
36.	University／学校（大学）	107
37.	Grades／成績	110
38.	Tests／試験	113
39.	Extracurricular Activities／課外活動	116
40.	Research & Development／調査・研究	119

[5] Art & Hobbies／芸術・趣味

41. **Music**／音楽 ... 122
42. **Visual Art**／絵画 ... 125
43. **Crafts**／工芸 ... 128
44. **Photography**／写真 ... 131
45. **Movies & Theater**／映画・演劇 ... 134
46. **Skills Acquisition**／芸道 ... 137
47. **Art in General**／芸術一般 ... 140
48. **Hobbies**／趣味 ... 143
49. **Collections**／コレクション ... 146
50. **DIY**／日曜大工 ... 149
51. **Handicraft**／手芸 ... 152
52. **Gambling**／ギャンブル ... 155
53. **Games**／遊び・ゲーム ... 158

[6] Religion & Festivals／宗教・祭り

54. **Religion**／宗教 ... 161
55. **Festivals**／祭り ... 164

[7] History／歴史

56. **History**／歴史 ... 167

[8] Media／メディア

57. **Media**／メディア ... 170
58. **Show Business**／芸能界 ... 173

[9] Telecommunications & Computers／通信・コンピュータ

59. **Telecommunications**／通信 ... 176
60. **Computers**／コンピュータ ... 179

[10] The Economy & Consumption／経済・消費

61. Shopping & Family Finance／買い物・家計 ... 182
62. Work／労働 ... 185
63. Job Hunting／就職活動 ... 188
64. Business／ビジネス ... 191
65. Stocks／株 ... 194
66. Economy & Finance／経済・財政・金融 ... 197
67. International Finance／国際経済・金融 ... 200
68. Taxes／税 ... 203

[11] Industry／産業

69. Industry in General／工業一般 ... 206
70. The Automobile Industry／自動車産業 ... 209
71. Heavy Industry／重工業 ... 212
72. Light Industry／軽工業・機械工業 ... 215
73. Construction & Engineering／建設・土木 ... 218
74. Energy／エネルギー ... 221
75. Agriculture & Forestry／農林業 ... 224
76. The Fishing Industry／水産業 ... 227

[12] Society／社会

77. Accidents／事件・事故 ... 230
78. Discrimination／差別 ... 233
79. Aging Society & Falling Birthrate／少子高齢化 ... 236
80. Social Security & Welfare／社会保障・福祉 ... 239

[13] Politics／政治

- 81. Politics／政治 ... 242
- 82. Law／法律 ... 245
- 83. Social Movements／社会運動 ... 248
- 84. Elections／選挙 ... 251
- 85. Diplomacy／外交 ... 254
- 86. War／戦争 ... 257
- 87. Conferences & Meetings／会議 ... 260

[14] Mankind & Living Things／ヒト・生き物

- 88. The Human Body／人体 ... 263
- 89. Medical Treatment／医療 ... 266
- 90. Health & Beauty／美容・健康 ... 269
- 91. Animals／動物 ... 272
- 92. Plants／植物 ... 275

[15] Nature／自然

- 93. Weather／気象 ... 278
- 94. Nature & Geographical Features／自然・地勢 ... 281
- 95. Disaster／災害 ... 284
- 96. The Earth's Environment／環境問題 ... 287
- 97. Space／宇宙 ... 290

[16] Science／サイエンス

- 98. Mathematics／算数・数学 ... 293
- 99. Science／サイエンス ... 296
- 100. Technology／テクノロジー ... 299

音声データダウンロードの方法

① PC・スマートフォンで音声ダウンロード用のサイトにアクセスします。

QRコード読み取りアプリを起動し、以下のQRコードを読み取ってください。

QRコードが読み取れない方はブラウザから「http://febe.jp/hituzi」にアクセスしてください。

② 表示されたページから、audiobook.jp への登録ページに進みます。

※音声のダウンロードには、audiobook.jpへの会員登録(無料)が必要です。

③ 登録後、シリアルコードの入力欄に「68581」を入力して「送信」をクリックします。

④ 「ライブラリに追加」のボタンをタップします。

⑤ スマートフォンの場合はアプリ「audiobook.jp」の案内が出ますので、アプリからご利用ください。

PCの場合は、「ライブラリ」から音声ファイルをダウンロードしてご利用ください。

<ご注意>

・PCからでも、iPhoneやAndroidのスマートフォンからでも音声を再生いただけます。
・音声は何度でもダウンロード・再生いただくことができます。
・ダウンロードについてのお問い合わせ先:info@febe.jp (受付時間:平日の10~20時)

英語ナレーター David Neale
MAI

脱 文法

100トピック
実践英語
トレーニング

1. Clothing
衣

❖ 質問しよう

A1 あなたはファッションに興味がありますか。
Are you interested in fashion?

A2 あなたは新しいファッションについてどうやって知りますか。
How do you learn about new fashions?

B1 あなたの好きな服装について話してください。
Would you describe your favorite outfit?

❖ 答えよう

A1 Are you interested in fashion?
はい。// いいえ。// はい、あります。// いいえ、ありません。// あまり。
Yes. // No. // Yes, I am. // No, I'm not. // Not so much.

A2 How do you learn about new fashions?
私はいつもテレビやインターネットを通してファッションについて知ります。// 私はよく有名人が着ているものを真似します。
I usually learn about fashion through TV or the Internet. // I often imitate what celebrities wear.

B1 Would you describe your favorite outfit?
①私はカジュアルなファッションが本当に好きです。
I really like casual fashion.

②私の好きな服装は、黒のTシャツ、ジーンズに黒のスニーカーです。
My favorite outfit is a black t-shirt, a pair of jeans and a pair of black sneakers.

③私がこの服装をする時、私はくつろぎと安らぎを感じます。
When I wear this outfit, I feel relaxed and comfortable.

④私は、人々が本当の私を見ることができると思います。
　I think people can see the real me.
⑤もっとフォーマルなものを着る時には、私は自分らしいとは感じません。
　When I wear something more formal, I don't feel like myself.

❖ 練習しよう：❶ 単語ごとに英訳しよう
　　　　　　　　❷「/」ごとに英訳しよう

B1 Would you describe your favorite outfit?

①私　本当に　好きだ　/カジュアルな　ファッション。
　I really like / casual fashion.

②私の　好きな　服装　だ　/1つの　黒い　Tシャツ
　My favorite outfit is / a black t-shirt,

　/1つの　ペア　の　ジーンズ
　/ a pair of jeans

　/そして　1つの　ペア　の　黒い　スニーカー。
　/ and a pair of black sneakers.

③時　私　着る　この　服装
　When I wear this outfit,

　/私　感じる　リラックスしている
　/ I feel relaxed

　/そして　快適だ。
　/ and comfortable.

④私　思う　/人々　できる　見る　/その　本当の　私。
　I think / people can see / the real me.

⑤時　私　着る　/何か　より　フォーマル
　When I wear / something more formal,

　/私　ない　感じる　/ようだ　自分自身。
　/ I don't feel / like myself.

1 Clothing 衣

❖ 覚えよう

B1 **Would you describe your favorite outfit?**

I really like casual fashion. My favorite outfit is a black t-shirt, a pair of jeans and a pair of black sneakers. When I wear this outfit, I feel relaxed and comfortable. I think people can see the real me. When I wear something more formal, I don't feel like myself.

❖ 話してみよう

A1 What is your favorite place to buy clothes?

A2 What kind of clothes do you wear when you feel happy?

B1 How can clothing influence people's opinions about you?

2 Food
食

❖ 質問しよう

> **A1** あなたの好きな食べ物は何ですか。
> What's your favorite food?
>
> **A2** あなたはどのくらいの頻度で料理をしますか。
> How often do you cook?
>
> **B1** あなたの好きな料理の作り方を話してもらえますか。
> Could you tell me how to make your favorite dish?

❖ 答えよう

A1 What's your favorite food?

カレーライスです。// カレーライスだと思います。

Curry and rice. // Curry and rice, I guess.

A2 How often do you cook?

毎日料理をします。// 週2回料理をします。// 料理はめったにしません。

I cook every day. // I cook twice a week. // I rarely cook.

B1 Could you tell me how to make your favorite dish?

①カレーライスの作り方を話します。

I'll tell you how to make curry and rice.

②中サイズのジャガイモ2個、玉ねぎ2個、人参1本、豚の薄切り約200グラム、そしてカレールーが1つ必要です。

You'll need two medium-sized potatoes, two onions, one carrot, about 200 grams of sliced pork and a bar of curry stock.

③まずジャガイモ、人参、玉ねぎを角切りにします。

First cut the potatoes, carrot and onions into cubes.

④それから深い鍋に少しサラダ油をひいて、豚の薄切りを炒めます。
Then pour a little vegetable oil into a deep pan and fry the sliced pork.

⑤そのあと、切った野菜を加えます。
After that, mix in the chopped vegetables.

⑥野菜が半生になったら、水2カップを加えて、野菜が柔らかくなるまで煮込みます。
When the vegetables are half-cooked, add two cups of water and let it simmer until the vegetables are done.

⑦最後にカレールーを加えて、ルーがすべて溶けるまでかき回します。
Finally, add the bar of curry stock and stir until it dissolves.

❖ 練習しよう：❶ 単語ごとに英訳しよう　❷「 / 」ごとに英訳しよう

B1 **Could you tell me how to make your favorite dish?**

①私だろう　言う　あなたに　/どうやって　作ること　カレーライス。
I'll tell you / how to make curry and rice.

②あなただろう　必要だ　/2つの　ミディアムサイズの　ジャガイモ
You'll need / two medium-sized potatoes,

/2つの　玉ねぎ　/1つの　人参　/約　200グラム　の　スライスポーク
/ two onions, / one carrot, / about 200 grams of sliced pork

/そして　1つの　バー　の　カレーストック。
/ and a bar of curry stock.

③最初に　/切る　その　ポテト　/人参　/そして　玉ねぎ
First / cut the potatoes, / carrot / and onions

/の中に　キューブ。
/ into cubes.

④それから　/そそぐ　少しの　野菜オイル　/の中に　1つの　深い　なべ
Then / pour a little vegetable oil / into a deep pan

/そして　炒める　/その　スライスポーク。
/ and fry / the sliced pork.

⑤後で その ／混ぜる 中に ／その 刻まれた 野菜。
After that, / mix in / the chopped vegetables.

⑥時 その 野菜 だ 半分料理される ／加える 2カップ の 水
When the vegetables are half-cooked, / add two cups of water

／そして させる それを 煮える ／まで その 野菜 だ される。
/ and let it simmer / until the vegetables are done.

⑦最後に ／加える その バー の カレーストック
Finally, / add the bar of curry stock

／そして かき混ぜる ／まで それ 溶ける。
/ and stir / until it dissolves.

❖ 覚えよう

B1 **Could you tell me how to make your favorite dish?**

I'll tell you how to make curry and rice. You'll need two medium-sized potatoes, two onions, one carrot, about 200 grams of sliced pork and a bar of curry stock. First cut the potatoes, carrot and onions into cubes. Then pour a little vegetable oil into a deep pan and fry the sliced pork. After that, mix in the chopped vegetables. When the vegetables are half-cooked, add two cups of water and let it simmer until the vegetables are done. Finally, add the bar of curry stock and stir until it dissolves.

❖ 話してみよう

A1 What's your favorite restaurant?
A2 How often do you eat out?
B1 Would you describe a perfect meal at a restaurant?

3 Alcohol
酒

❖ 質問しよう

A1 あなたの国では何歳からお酒が飲めますか。
What is the drinking age in your country?

A2 あなたの国で人々がお酒を飲む典型的な行事は何ですか。
What are some typical events where people drink alcohol in your country?

B1 なぜ人々はお酒を飲むのだと思いますか。
Why do you think people drink alcohol?

❖ 答えよう

A1 What is the drinking age in your country?
20歳です。// 20歳です。
Twenty-years old. // Twenty.

A2 What are some typical events where people drink alcohol in your country?
新年会や夏祭りなどの人が集まるイベントでお酒を飲みます。結婚式などのお祝い事でもお酒を飲みます。
We drink alcohol at social events, such as New Year's parties and summer festivals. We drink when we celebrate things like weddings, too.

B1 Why do you think people drink alcohol?
①日本では主に2つの理由でお酒を飲みます。
I think people drink alcohol for two main reasons in Japan.

②まず、友達、同僚あるいは上司と親交を深めるためです。
The first is to socialize with friends, colleagues or even our bosses.

③お酒をともにすることで人間関係が深まると私たちは考えます。
We believe drinking alcohol together strengthens human relationships.

④2つめの理由は宗教に関連しています。
The second reason relates to religion.

⑤お酒は我々の魂を清めると考えているので、新しいことを始める際にはお酒を飲みます。
People believe *sake* purifies our souls, so we drink it when we start a new project.

❖ 練習しよう：❶ 単語ごとに英訳しよう　❷「 / 」ごとに英訳しよう

B1 Why do you think people drink alcohol?

①私　思う　/ 人々　飲む　アルコール　/ のため　2つの　主な　理由
I think / people drink alcohol / for two main reasons

/ に　日本。
/ in Japan.

②その　最初　だ　/ ため　友好を深める　一緒に　友達　/ 同僚
The first is / to socialize with friends, / colleagues

/ または　さえ　私たちの　上司。
/ or even our bosses.

③私たち　信じる　/ 飲むこと　アルコール　ともに
We believe / drinking alcohol together

/ 強める　人間　関係。
/ strengthens human relationships.

④その　2番目の　理由　/ 関係する　に　宗教。
The second reason / relates to religion.

⑤人々　信じる　/ 酒　清める　私たちの　魂
People believe / *sake* purifies our souls,

/ だから　私たち　飲む　それ　/ 時　私たち　始める
/ so we drink it / when we start

/1つの 新しい プロジェクト。
/ a new project.

❖ 覚えよう

B1 **Why do you think people in Japan drink alcohol?**

I think people drink alcohol for two main reasons in Japan. The first is to socialize with friends, colleagues or even our bosses. We believe drinking alcohol together strengthens human relationships. The second reason relates to religion. People believe *sake* purifies our souls, so we drink it when we start a new project.

❖ 話してみよう

A1 What is the most popular alcoholic drink in your country?

A2 Where do people usually drink alcohol in your country?

B1 What are some positive and negative points about drinking alcohol?

4 Travel
旅行

❖ 質問しよう

A1 あなたは日本でどこを旅したことがありますか。
Where have you traveled in Japan?

A2 あなたは日本のどんな場所を訪れることを勧めますか。
What places do you recommend visiting in Japan?

B1 日本であなたの好きな休暇場所を話してください。
Would you describe your favorite vacation spot in Japan?

❖ 答えよう

A1 Where have you traveled in Japan?
京都と奈良、それから北海道のいくつかの場所です。
Kyoto, Nara, and a few places in Hokkaido.

A2 What places do you recommend visiting in Japan?
京都を勧めます。紅葉が古いお寺に合うので、秋に京都を訪れるべきです。
I recommend Kyoto. You should visit Kyoto in the fall since the autumn leaves really look nice with the old temples.

B1 Would you describe your favorite vacation spot in Japan?
①日本で私の好きなスポットは琵琶湖です。
My favorite spot in Japan is Biwako.

②琵琶湖あるいはLake Biwaは、京都に近い日本のど真ん中に位置しています。
Biwako, or Lake Biwa, is located in the center of Japan close to Kyoto.

③琵琶湖は日本で最大の湖であり、北から南に伸びているので、この独特な地理的特徴により、たくさんの興味深い経験ができます。
Since it is the largest lake in Japan and stretches from north to south, this unique geographic feature gives us a lot of

4 Travel 旅行

interesting experiences.

④例えば、快晴と降雪を一時間以内に見ることができます。

For example, we can see sunshine and falling snow in a single hour.

⑤晴れた日に京都から電車に乗れば、40分後には、近江舞子駅で雪を見ることができます。

If you take the train from Kyoto on a sunny day, 40 minutes later at Oumi Maiko Station you may see snow.

❖ 練習しよう：❶ 単語ごとに英訳しよう
❷「／」ごとに英訳しよう

B1 Would you describe your favorite vacation spot in Japan?

①私の　好きな　スポット　／に　日本　／だ　琵琶湖。

My favorite spot / in Japan / is Biwako.

②琵琶湖　／または　湖　琵琶　／は　位置している

Biwako, / or Lake Biwa, / is located

／に　その　真ん中　の　日本　／近い　に　京都。

/ in the center of Japan, / close to Kyoto.

③ので　／それ　だ　その　最大の　湖　／に　日本　／そして　伸びる

Since / it is the largest lake / in Japan / and stretches

／から　北　に　南　／この　独特な　地理的な　特徴　／与える　私たち

/ from north to south, / this unique geographic feature / gives us

／たくさんの　興味深い　経験。

/ a lot of interesting experiences.

④例えば　／私たち　できる　見る　太陽光　／そして　降っている　雪

For example, /we can see sunshine / and falling snow

／に　1つの　単一の　時間。

/ in a single hour.

⑤もし　あなた　とる　／その　列車　から　京都

If you take / the train from Kyoto

/に 1つの 天気のいい 日 /40分 後 /に 近江舞子駅
/ on a sunny day, / 40 minutes later / at Oumi Maiko Station

/あなた かもしれない 見る 雪。
/ you may see snow.

❖ 覚えよう

B1 **Would you describe your favorite vacation spot in Japan?**

My favorite spot in Japan is Biwako. Biwako, or Lake Biwa, is located in the center of Japan, close to Kyoto. Since it is the largest lake in Japan and stretches from north to south, this unique geographic feature gives us a lot of interesting experiences. For example, we can see sunshine and falling snow in a single hour. If you take the train from Kyoto on a sunny day, 40 minutes later at Oumi Maiko Station, you may see snow.

❖ 話してみよう

> **A1** Which place would you like to visit overseas?
> **A2** What would you like to do if you traveled to another country?
> **B1** Why do you want to travel to another country?

5 Sports
スポーツ

❖ 質問しよう

> **A1** あなたは何かスポーツチームのファンですか。
> Are you a fan of any sports teams?
>
> **A2** あなたの高校で最も人気のあったスポーツは何ですか。
> What sport was the most popular at your high school?
>
> **B1** どの有名スポーツ選手が立派だと思いますか。それはなぜですか。
> Which famous professional athlete do you admire and why?

❖ 答えよう

A1 **Are you a fan of any sports teams?**
はい。// いいえ。// あまり。
Yes. // No. // Not really.

A2 **What sport was the most popular at your high school?**
私たちの高校では野球がとても人気がありました。なぜなら春と夏に全国大会があり、テレビで放送されるからです。

Baseball was a very popular sport at our high school because we have a huge national championship in spring and summer, which is broadcast nationally.

B1 **Which famous professional athlete do you admire and why?**
①私はイチローが立派だと思います。なぜなら彼は、メジャーリーグの野球選手になるために非常に大きな努力をしました。そして、彼はそれを成し遂げました。

I admire Ichiro because he made great efforts to become a major league baseball player, and he accomplished that.

②彼は常に高い目標を自分自身で設定して、そして彼の独自の方法でそれを成し遂げようとします。

He always sets a high goal for himself and tries to achieve it in his own way.

③彼は自分自身にも厳しいです。
He is also very disciplined.

④例えば、彼は試合の前後や最中にストレッチをするので、その結果、けがを防いでいるのです。
For example, he always stretches before, during and after a game and, as a result, avoids injuries.

⑤だから私はイチローを立派だと思います。
That is why I admire Ichiro.

❖ 練習しよう：❶ 単語ごとに英訳しよう
　　　　　　　❷「／」ごとに英訳しよう

B1 Which famous professional athlete do you admire and why?

①私　賞賛する　／イチロー　／なぜなら　彼　作った　大きい　努力
I admire Ichiro / because he made great efforts

／ため　なる　1つの　メジャーリーグ　野球　選手
/ to become a major league baseball player,

／そして　／彼は　成し遂げた　それ。
/ and, / he accomplished that.

②彼　いつも　設定する　／1つの　高い　ゴール　／のために　彼自身
He always sets / a high goal / for himself

／そして　試みる　／ため　成し遂げる　それ　／に　彼の　自身の　方法。
/ and tries / to achieve it / in his own way.

③彼　だ　また　とても　鍛錬されている。
He is also / very disciplined.

④例えば　／彼　いつも　ストレッチする　／前　間
For example, / he always stretches / before, during

／そして　後　1つの　ゲーム　／そして　結果として　／避ける　けが。
/ and after a game / and, as a result, / avoids injuries.

⑤それ　だ　なぜ　／私　称賛する　イチロー。
That is why / I admire Ichiro.

❖ 覚えよう

B1 Which famous professional athlete do you admire and why?

I admire Ichiro because he made great efforts to become a major league baseball player, and he accomplished that. He always sets a high goal for himself and tries to achieve it in his own way. He is also very disciplined. For example, he always stretches before, during and after a game and, as a result, avoids injuries. That is why I admire Ichiro.

❖ 話してみよう

> A1 Do you like to play sports?
> A2 Why do people play sports?
> B1 Could you explain the basic rules of a sport that you know?

6 Housing
住

❖ 質問しよう

> **A1** あなたはあなたの家にどのくらいの期間住んでいますか。
> How long have you lived in your home?
>
> **A2** あなたの家で最も安らげる場所はどこですか。
> What is the most comfortable place in your home?
>
> **B1** あなたの夢の家はどんな家ですか。
> What would your dream house be like?

❖ 答えよう

A1 How long have you lived in your home?
18年です。// 約18年です。//18年ぐらいです。
Eighteen years. // About eighteen years. // Eighteen years or so.

A2 What is the most comfortable place in your home?
私の家で最も心地よい場所は間違いなくソファです。私はそこに座り、テレビを見て、家族と時間を過ごすことが好きです。
The most comfortable place in my home is definitely the sofa. I like to sit there, watch TV, and spend time with my family.

B1 What would your dream house be like?
①私の夢の家は一種のエコハウスです。
My dream house would be a kind of eco-house.
②必要なすべての電気はソーラーパネルから得ます。
We would get all the electricity we need from solar panels.
③私たちが使う水のすべてはリサイクルします。
All of the water we use would be recycled.
④そしてすべての食べ物は庭で育てます。
And we would grow all of our own food in our garden.

⑤さらに、そこはとても快適です。
　At the same time, it would be very comfortable.
⑥ホームシアターとモダンなキッチンとサウナがあります。
　We would have a home theater, a modern kitchen and a sauna.
⑦それが私の夢の家です。
　This is my dream house.

❖ 練習しよう：❶ 単語ごとに英訳しよう
　　　　　　　 ❷「 / 」ごとに英訳しよう

B1 What would your dream house be like?
①私の　夢の　家　/だろう　だ　/一種の　エコハウス。
　My dream house / would be / a kind of eco-house.
②私たち　だろう　得る　/すべての　その　電気
　We would get / all the electricity

　/ 私たち　必要だ　/から　ソーラーパネル。
　/ we need / from solar panels.
③すべて　の　その　水　/私たち　使う
　All of the water / we use

　/だろう　だ　リサイクルされる。
　/ would be recycled.
④そして　私たち　だろう　育てる
　And we would grow

　/すべて　の　私たちの　自身の　食べ物　/に　私たちの　庭。
　/ all of our own food / in our garden.
⑤同時に　/それ　だろう　だ　とても　快適。
　At the same time, / it would be very comfortable.
⑥私たち　だろう　持つ　1つの　ホームシアター
　We would have a home theater,

　/1つの　モダンな　キッチン　/そして　1つの　サウナ。
　/ a modern kitchen / and a sauna.

⑦これ だ / 私の 夢の 家。
This is / my dream house.

❖ 覚えよう

B1 **What would your dream house be like?**

My dream house would be a kind of eco-house. We would get all the electricity we need from solar panels. All of the water we use would be recycled. And we would grow all of our own food in our garden. At the same time, it would be very comfortable. We would have a home theater, a modern kitchen and a sauna. This is my dream house.

❖ 話してみよう

> **A1** How often do you clean your room in a month?
> **A2** What do you like about your room?
> **B1** Would you describe your room in detail?

7 Languages
言葉

❖ 質問しよう

A1 最も美しい外国語は何だと思いますか。
What do you think is the most beautiful foreign language?

A2 外国人にとって日本語を学ぶ上で難しいポイントは何ですか。
What is one difficult point about learning Japanese for foreigners?

B1 しりとりのルールを説明してください。
Could you describe the game *shiritori*?

❖ 答えよう

A1 What do you think is the most beautiful foreign language?
スペイン語です。/ たぶんスペイン語です。
Spanish. // Maybe Spanish.

A2 What is one difficult point about learning Japanese for foreigners?
漢字あるいは中国語文字が、外国人にとって難しいポイントの1つだと思います。なぜならある漢字には様々な意味や様々な発音方法があるからです。
I think kanji, or Chinese characters, is one difficult point for a foreigner because some *kanji* have various meanings and various pronunciations.

B1 Could you describe the game *shiritori*?
①それは2人以上の間でする言葉遊びです。
It's a word game between two or more people.

②1人が単語を言って、次の人はその単語の最後の音で始まる単語を考えて言わなければなりません。
One person says one word and the next person has to say

another word that starts with the same sound that the first word ended with.

③例えば、もし最初の人が「バナナ」で始めたら、2番目の人は「なつ」と答えることができます。

For example, if the first person starts with the word "*banana*," then the second person could answer with "*natsu*."

④誰かが新しい単語を思いつかなくなるまで、単語を言い続けます。

You continue saying new words until someone can't think of a new word.

⑤あっ　それから、「ん」で終わる単語言ったら負けです。

Oh, and words that end with the sound "*n*" aren't allowed.

❖ 練習しよう：❶ 単語ごとに英訳しよう　　❷「／」ごとに英訳しよう

B1 Could you describe the game *shiritori*?

①それだ　1つの　言葉　ゲーム

It's a word game

／の間　2つの　または　より多い　人々。

/ between two or more people.

②1つの　人　言う　1つの　語　／そして　／その　次の　人

One person says one word / and / the next person

／なければならない　言う　もう1つの　語

/ has to say another word

／それ　スタートする　と一緒に　その　同じ　音

/ that starts with the same sound

／それ　その　最初の　語　終わった　と一緒に。

/ that the first word ended with.

③例えば　／もし　その　最初の　人　スタートする

For example, / if the first person starts

／と一緒に　その　語　バナナ　／それから

/ with the word "*banana*," / then

/ その　2番めの　人　できた　答える　/ と一緒に　夏。
/ the second person could answer / with "*natsu*."

④あなた　続ける　言うこと　新しい　語
You continue saying new words

/ まで　誰か　できない　考える　の　1つの　新しい　語。
/ until someone can't think of a new word.

⑤ああ　/ そして　語　それ　終わる　と一緒に　その　音　ん
Oh, / and words that end with the sound "*n*"

/ ない　許される。
/ aren't allowed.

❖ 覚えよう

B1 **Could you describe the game *shiritori*?**

It's a word game between two or more people. One person says one word and the next person has to say another word that starts with the same sound that the first word ended with. For example, if the first person starts with the word "*banana*," then the second person could answer with "*natsu*." You continue saying new words until someone can't think of a new word. Oh, and words that end with the sound "*n*" aren't allowed.

❖ 話してみよう

A1 Have you ever studied a foreign language aside from English?

A2 What is one of the benefits of learning another language?

B1 Could you describe an effective method for learning a new language?

8 Literature & Publications
文芸・出版

❖ 質問しよう

> **A1** あなたは漫画を読むことが好きですか
> Do you like to read manga?
>
> **A2** どの連載漫画があなたは一番好きですか。
> What manga series do you like the best?
>
> **B1** あなたが知っている漫画のキャラクターを説明してください。
> Would you describe a manga character you know?

❖ 答えよう

A1 Do you like to read manga?
はい。// いいえ。// あまり。// はい、漫画が好きです。
Yes. // No. // Not really. // Yes, I like manga.

A2 What manga series do you like the best?
私はドラえもんと呼ばれるシリーズが一番好きです。
I like the series called Doraemon the best.

B1 Would you describe a manga character you know?
①えー、ドラえもんについて話させてください。
Well, let me tell you about Doraemon.
②ドラえもんは未来から来たロボットです。
Doraemon is a robot that came from the future.
③彼は何でもほしいものが手に入る驚くべきポケットを持っています。
He has an amazing pocket that allows him to get anything he wants.

8 Literature & Publications 文芸・出版

④例えば、もし彼が外国語を話したいと思う時、彼はほんやくコンニャクと呼ばれるある食べ物を取り出します。それがあれば、彼が話したいと思うどんな言語でも話させてくれます。

For example, if he wants to speak a foreign language, he takes out some food called *honyaku konnyaku*, which lets him speak any language he wants to speak.

⑤ドラえもんは日本でとても人気があります。

Doraemon is very popular in Japan.

❖ 練習しよう：❶ 単語ごとに英訳しよう
　　　　　　 ❷「／」ごとに英訳しよう

B1 Would you describe a manga character you know?

①えー ／させる 私 言う あなた ／について ドラえもん。
Well, / let me tell you / about Doraemon.

②ドラえもん だ 1つの ロボット ／それ 来た から その 未来。
Doraemon is a robot / that came from the future.

③彼 持つ 1つの 驚くべき ポケット ／それ 許す 彼
He has an amazing pocket / that allows him

／得ること 何でも ／彼 ほしい。
/ to get anything / he wants.

④例えば ／もし 彼 ほしい 話すこと ／1つの 外国の 言語
For example, / if he wants to speak / a foreign language,

／彼 とる 外に いくつかの 食べ物 ／呼ばれる ほんやくコンニャク
/ he takes out some food / called *honyaku konnyaku*,

／それ させる 彼 話す ／どんな 言語 ／彼 ほしい 話すこと。
/ which lets him speak / any language / he wants to speak.

⑤ドラえもん だ とても 人気がある ／に 日本。
Doraemon is very popular / in Japan.

❖ 覚えよう

B1 Would you describe a manga character you know?

Well, let me tell you about Doraemon. Doraemon is a robot that came from the future. He has an amazing pocket that allows him to get anything he wants. For example, if he wants to speak a foreign language, he takes out some food called *honyaku konnyaku*, which lets him speak any language he wants to speak. Doraemon is very popular in Japan.

❖ 話してみよう

> A1 Do you like to read?
> A2 Who is your favorite author and why?
> B1 Could you describe your favorite book?

Seasons & Events
季節・行事

❖ 質問しよう

A1 あなたは夏祭りに行くことが好きですか。
Do you like going to summer festivals?

A2 お盆の間あなたはいつも何をしますか。
What do you usually do over *O-bon*?

B1 あなたは新年をどのように祝いますか。
How do you celebrate the new year?

❖ 答えよう

A1 Do you like going to summer festivals?
はい。// あまり。// あまり。
Yes. // No. // Not so much.

A2 What do you usually do over *O-bon*?
私は夜いつも浴衣を着て、それから地元の夏祭りに行きます。そして焼きそばなどの地元の食べ物を食べます。
I usually wear *yukata* one night and then go to the local summer festival and have some nice local food like fried noodles.

B1 How do you celebrate the new year?
①私は家族と新年を祝います。
I celebrate the new year with my family.

②大みそかには、たくさんの音楽パフォーマンスを見られる紅白と呼ばれるテレビ番組を見ます。
On New Year's Eve, we watch a TV show called *Kouhaku* that has a lot of musical performances.

③それは日本でとても人気がある番組です。
It's a very popular program in Japan.

④元旦には、おせちと呼ばれる特別な食べ物を食べます。
On New Year's Day, we eat special food called *osechi*.

⑤おせち料理はいくつかの異なる種類の食べ物で構成されていて、その1つひとつの食べ物には、長寿やたくさんお金が稼げるなど、意味があります。
Osechi consists of some different kinds of food and each food has a meaning, like having a long life, or earning a lot of money.

⑥それから、元旦には新年の幸運を祈念するために、いつも家族と神社に行きます。
Oh, and my family and I always go to a shrine to pray for good luck in the new year.

❖ 練習しよう：❶ 単語ごとに英訳しよう
    ❷「 / 」ごとに英訳しよう

B1 How do you celebrate the new year?

①私は 祝う その 新年 /と一緒に 私の 家族。
I celebrate the new year / with my family.

②に 大晦日 / 私たち 見る 1つの テレビショー / 呼ばれる 紅白
On New Year's Eve, / we watch a TV show / called *Kouhaku*

/それ 持つ たくさんの ミュージカルパフォーマンス。
/ that has a lot of musical performances.

③それだ 1つの とても 人気がある 番組 /中で 日本。
It's a very popular program / in Japan.

④に 元旦 / 私たち 食べる 特別な 食べ物 /呼ばれる おせち。
On New Year's Day, / we eat special food / called *osechi*.

⑤おせちは 成り立つ の /いくつかの 異なる 種類 の 食べ物
Osechi consists of / some different kinds of food

/そして それぞれの 食べ物 持つ /1つの 意味
/ and each food has / a meaning,

/ような 持つこと 1つの 長い 人生
/ like having a long life,

/または 稼ぐこと たくさんの お金。
/ or earning a lot of money.

⑥ああ /そして 私の 家族 /そして 私 いつも /行く に 神社
Oh, / and my family / and I always / go to a shrine

/ため 祈る のために 幸運 /に その 新しい 年。
/ to pray for good luck / in the new year.

❖ 覚えよう

B1 **How do you celebrate the new year?**

I celebrate the new year with my family. On New Year's Eve, we watch a TV show called *Kouhaku* that has a lot of musical performances. It's a very popular program in Japan. On New Year's Day, we eat special food called *osechi*. *Osechi* consists of some different kinds of food and each food has a meaning, like having a long life, or earning a lot of money. Oh, and my family and I always go to a shrine to pray for good luck in the new year.

❖ 話してみよう

> **A1** What is your favorite season?
> **A2** In which season is it best to visit Japan?
> **B1** What are the good points of your favorite season?

10 Culture in General
文化一般

❖ 質問しよう

> **A1** 外国へ行ったことがありますか。
> Have you ever been to a foreign country?
>
> **A2** 他の国々の人々が日本を訪れたいと思うのはなぜだと思いますか。
> Why do you think people from other countries like to visit Japan?
>
> **B1** 旅からあなたは何を学ぶことができますか。
> What can you learn from traveling?

❖ 答えよう

A1 Have you ever been to a foreign country?

はい、アメリカです。// はい。// いいえ。// 1度も。// はい、あります。// いいえ、ありません。

Yes, the United States. // Yes. // No. // Never. // Yes, I have. // No, I haven't.

A2 Why do you think people from other countries like to visit Japan?

オタク文化を経験するために秋葉原に行くことを好む人がいます。また、私たちの伝統的な習慣や、京都や鎌倉にあるお寺のような建造物に興味を持つ人もいます。

Some people like to go to Akihabara to experience *Otaku* culture. Other people are interested in our traditional customs and buildings, such as the temples in Kyoto or Kamakura.

B1 What can you learn from traveling?

①私はいつも旅をするとだいたい3つのことを学びます。

I usually learn about three things when I travel.

②まず、地元の食べ物です。
The first thing is the local food.

③私は地元の食べ物を味会うことが本当に好きです。だから私は旅をする時はそれをいつも探します。
I really like tasting local food so I always look for it when I travel.

④2つめは地元の文化です。人々がエスカレーターでどう並ぶかなどという些細なことでさえ興味があります。
The second thing is the local culture—even small things like how people line up for the escalator.

⑤3つめは言葉です。
The third thing is the language.

⑥私はだいたい「こんにちは」「ありがとう」そして「これはいくらですか」という言葉を学習するように心がけています。
I usually try to learn some basic phrases like, "Hello," "Thank you," "How much is this?" and things like that.

❖ 練習しよう：❶ 単語ごとに英訳しよう
❷「／」ごとに英訳しよう

B1 What can you learn from traveling?

①私は 通常 学ぶ ／について 3つの こと ／時 私 旅する。
I usually learn ／ about three things ／ when I travel.

②その 最初の こと だ ／その 地元の 食べ物。
The first thing is ／ the local food.

③私は 本当に 好きだ ／味わうこと 地元の 食べ物
I really like ／ tasting local food

／だから ／私 いつも 探す それ ／時 私 旅する。
／ so ／ I always look for it ／ when I travel.

④その 2つめの こと だ ／その 地元の 文化 ／さえ 小さい こと
The second thing is ／ the local culture ／ —even small things

／ような ／どのように 人々 並ぶ ／のために その エスカレーター。
／ like ／ how people line up ／ for the escalator.

⑤その 3つめの こと だ /その 言語。
The third thing is / the language.

⑥私 普段 トライする 学ぶこと /いくつかの 基本的な フレーズ
I usually try to learn / some basic phrases

/ような /「こんにちは」 /「ありがとう」 /「これはいくらですか」
/ like, / "Hello," / "Thank you," / "How much is this?"

/そして こと ような それ。
/ and things like that.

❖ 覚えよう

B1 **What can you learn from traveling?**

I usually learn about three things when I travel. The first thing is the local food. I really like tasting local food so I always look for it when I travel. The second thing is the local culture—even small things like how people line up for the escalator. The third thing is the language. I usually try to learn some basic phrases like, "Hello," "Thank you," "How much is this?" and things like that.

❖ 話してみよう

A1 Have you ever met a foreigner?
A2 When and where did you meet a foreigner?
B1 Could you describe a cultural difference you have felt?

11 City Life
町

❖ 質問しよう

A1 あなたが住んでいる町で大好きな地域はどこですか。
What's your favorite area in your town?

A2 小さい町と比べて大都市に住む利点は何ですか。
What is a good point about living in a big city over a small town?

B1 あなたは東京に来た外国人をどこに連れて行ってあげたいですか。
What places would you take a foreign visitor to in Tokyo?

❖ 答えよう

A1 What's your favorite area in your town?
渋谷だと思います。// 渋谷です。
Shibuya, I guess. // Shibuya.

A2 What is a good point about living in a big city over a small town?
小さい町と比べて大都市に住む大きな利点は主な利点は、ほとんどどこにでも簡単にアクセスできることです。
The main advantage of living in a big city, instead of a small town, is the easy access you have to almost anywhere.

B1 What places would you take a foreign visitor to in Tokyo?

①私は訪れた人を3つの場所に連れていきたいです。
I would take a visitor to three places.

②まず伝統的な日本と近代日本のギャップを見せるために、明治神宮と原宿のようなその周辺の場所に連れて行きたいです。
First, I would take them to Meiji Shrine and the surrounding areas, like Harajuku, to show the gap between traditional Japan and modern Japan.

③2つめは、東京の下町の雰囲気を味わえる浅草の周辺に連れて行きたいです。

Second, I would like to show them around Asakusa, where people can get a taste of downtown Tokyo.

④3つめは、彼らを高尾山に連れて行きたいです。そこでは、東京であるにもかかわらず自然の豊かさを経験できます。

Third, I would take them to Mt. Takao, where people can experience the richness of nature even in Tokyo.

❖ 練習しよう：❶ 単語ごとに英訳しよう
❷「／」ごとに英訳しよう

B1 What places would you take a foreign visitor to in Tokyo?

①私　だろう　連れて行く　1人の　訪問者　／に　3つの　場所。
I would take a visitor / to three places.

②最初に　／私　だろう　連れて行く　彼ら　／に　明治神宮
First, / I would take them / to Meiji Shrine

／そして　その　まわりの　エリア　／ような　原宿
/ and the surrounding areas, / like Harajuku,

／ため　見せる　その　ギャップ　／の間　伝統的な　日本
/ to show the gap / between traditional Japan

／そして　近代的な　日本。
/and modern Japan.

③2つめに　／私　たい　見せる　彼ら　／まわり　浅草
Second, / I would like to show them / around Asakusa,

／そこで　人々　できる　得る　／1つの　テイスト　の　下町　東京。
/ where people can get / a taste of downtown Tokyo.

④3つめに　／私　だろう　連れて行く　彼ら　／に　高尾山
Third, / I would take them / to Mt. Takao,

／そこで　人々　できる　経験する　／その　豊かさ　の　自然
/ where people can experience / the richness of nature

/ さえ に 東京。
/ even in Tokyo.

❖ 覚えよう

B1 What places would you take a foreign visitor to in Tokyo?

I would take a visitor to three places. First, I would take them to Meiji Shrine and the surrounding areas, like Harajuku, to show the gap between traditional Japan and modern Japan. Second, I would like to show them around Asakusa, where people can get a taste of downtown Tokyo. Third, I would take them to Mt. Takao, where people can experience the richness of nature even in Tokyo.

❖ 話してみよう

A1 Are you from a big city?
A2 What are some famous big cities around the world?
B1 Which city in the world would you most like to visit, and why?

12 Hometown
ふるさと

❖ 質問しよう

A1 あなたの出身は日本のどこですか。
What part of Japan are you from?

A2 あなたの故郷のよい点は何ですか。
What is a good point about your hometown?

B1 あなたの故郷について話してください。
How would you describe your hometown?

❖ 答えよう

A1 What part of Japan are you from?
東京。// 東京出身です。
Tokyo. // From Tokyo.

A2 What is a good point about your hometown?
そこは、都市の生活とそしていくつかのハイキングと魚釣りのポイントへのよいアクセスができます。
It has good access to both city life and some nice hiking and fishing spots.

B1 How would you describe your hometown?
①私の故郷は八王子です。
My hometown is Hachioji.

②八王子について1つのいいところは、都市の生活とアウトドアの両方が楽しめるところです。
A good point about Hachioji is that we can enjoy both city life and outdoor activities.

③例えば、私たちはショッピングモールと美しい山の景色を楽しめる高尾山に簡単に行くことができます。
For example, we can easily go to a shopping mall and Mt. Takao, where we can enjoy beautiful mountain scenery.

④八王子には、両方の最高の場所があると言えます。
You could say that we have the best of both worlds in Hachioji.

❖ 練習しよう：❶ 単語ごとに英訳しよう
　　　　　　　❷「/」ごとに英訳しよう

B1 How would you describe your hometown?

①私の　故郷　だ　八王子。
My hometown is Hachioji.

②1つの　よい　ポイント　について　八王子　だ
A good point about Hachioji is

/ ということ　私たち　できる　楽しむ　/ 両方　シティライフ
/ that we can enjoy / both city life

/ と　アウトドア　活動。
/ and outdoor activities.

③例えば　/ 私たち　できる　簡単に
For example, / we can easily

/ 行く　に　1つの　ショッピングモール
/ go to a shopping mall

/ そして　高尾山　/ そこで　私たち　できる　楽しむ
/ and Mt. Takao, / where we can enjoy

/ 美しい　山　景色。
/ beautiful mountain scenery.

④あなた　できた　言う　/ ということ　私たち　持つ
You could say / that we have

/ その　ベスト　の　両方の　世界　に　八王子。
/ the best of both worlds / in Hachioji.

❖ 覚えよう

B1 **How would you describe your hometown?**

My hometown is Hachioji. A good point about Hachioji is that we can enjoy both city life and outdoor activities. For example, we can easily go to a shopping mall and Mt. Takao, where we can enjoy beautiful mountain scenery. You could say that we have the best of both worlds in Hachioji.

❖ 話してみよう

> **A1** Do you like your hometown?
> **A2** What are the people in your hometown like?
> **B1** What would be one way to improve your hometown?

13 Transportation
交通

❖ 質問しよう

> **A1** あなたは大学へどうやって来ますか。
> How do you get to your university?
>
> **A2** 電車に乗っている時どんなことをするのが好きですか。
> What do you like to do when you ride the train?
>
> **B1** あなたが学校に来る方法を順番に説明してください。
> Could you describe, step-by-step, how you come to the university?

❖ 答えよう

A1 **How do you get to your university?**
バスと電車です。// 私は歩きます。// 自転車です。
By bus and train. // I walk. // By bicycle.

A2 **What do you like to do when you ride the train?**
私は電車で音楽を聴いたり本を読んだりするのが好きです。
I usually like to listen to music and read books on the train.

B1 **Could you describe, step-by-step, how you come to the university?**

①まず最初に、地元の駅に10分かけて歩きます。

First of all, I walk for ten minutes to the local train station.

②それから、横浜線に乗って八王子に行きます。そして中央線に乗り換えて、新宿に行きます。

Then I take the Yokohama Line to Hachioji and change to the Chuo Line, which takes me to Shinjuku station.

③そこで山手線に乗り換えて2駅行くと渋谷です。

I then change to the Yamanote Line and go two stops to Shibuya.

④そこから、私は 10 分かけて大学まで歩きます。
　From there, I walk ten minutes to the university.
⑤ドア・トゥ・ドアで、約 1 時間半かかります。
　It takes about an hour and a half, door to door.

❖ 練習しよう：❶ 単語ごとに英訳しよう
　　　　　　　❷「／」ごとに英訳しよう

B1 Could you describe, step-by-step, how you come to the university?

①最初　の　すべて　／私　歩く　間　10 分
　First of all, / I walk for ten minutes

／に　その　地元の　列車　駅。
／ to the local train station.

②それから　／私　とる　その　横浜線　／に　八王子
　Then / I take the Yokohama Line / to Hachioji

／そして　乗り換える　に　その　中央線　／それ　連れて行く　私
／ and change to the Chuo Line, / which takes me

／に　新宿駅。
／ to Shinjuku station.

③私　それから　／乗り換える　に　その　山手線
　I then / change to the Yamanote Line

／そして　行く　2つの　駅　／に　渋谷。
／ and go two stops / to Shibuya.

④から　そこ　／私　歩く　10 分　／に　その　大学。
　From there, / I walk ten minutes / to the university.

⑤それ　かかる　／だいたい　1時間　そして　1つの　半分
　It takes / about an hour and a half,

／ドア・トゥ・ドア。
／ door to door.

❖ 覚えよう

B1 **Could you describe, step-by-step, how you come to the university?**

First of all, I walk for ten minutes to the local train station. Then I take the Yokohama Line to Hachioji and change to the Chuo Line, which takes me to Shinjuku station. I then change to the Yamanote Line and go two stops to Shibuya. From there, I walk ten minutes to the university. It takes about an hour and a half, door to door.

❖ 話してみよう

A1 Do you have a car?

A2 Which do you prefer, traveling by train or bus?

B1 What would be the best way to improve public transportation in Tokyo?

14 Daily Life
日常生活

❖ 質問しよう

> **A1** あなたは暇な時に何をすることが好きですか。
> What do you like to do in your free time?
>
> **A2** 先週の週末は何をしましたか。
> What did you do last weekend?
>
> **B1** あなたの完璧な週末を説明してください。
> How would you describe your perfect weekend?

❖ 答えよう

A1 **What do you like to do in your free time?**
買いものか読書です。
Shopping or reading books.

A2 **What did you do last weekend?**
私は友達と一緒にショッピングへ行きました。
I went shopping with my friends.

B1 **How would you describe your perfect weekend?**
①私の完璧な週末は土曜日には家で1日中寝ています。

My perfect weekend would be sleeping at home all day on Saturday.

②というのは、平日はとても忙しいので、寝だめしたいからです。

This is because I am very busy during the week and I always want to catch up on my sleep.

③でも、起きた後は、普段美味しい食事をしたり長くおしゃべりしたりするために、友達と会うのが好きです。

After I wake up, though, I usually like to meet my friends for a nice meal and a long talk.

④日曜日は、遅くまで寝ません。
On Sunday, I wouldn't sleep too late.
⑤私はパンケーキのような美味しくてしっかりした朝食を食べます。
I'd have a nice big breakfast—something like pancakes.
⑥それから映画を見たり面白い本を読んだりします。
Then I'd watch movies or read an interesting book.
⑦これが私にとって完璧な週末です。
To me, this would be a perfect weekend.

❖ 練習しよう：❶ 単語ごとに英訳しよう
　　　　　　❷「 / 」ごとに英訳しよう

B1 **How would you describe your perfect weekend?**

①私の　完璧な　週末　だろう　だ　/寝ている　で　家　すべて　日
My perfect weekend would be / sleeping at home all day

/ に　土曜日。
/ on Saturday.

②これ　だ　なぜなら　/ 私　だ　とても　忙しい　/ 間　その　週
This is because / I am very busy / during the week

/ そして　私　いつも　ほしい　追いつくこと　/ に　私の　眠り。
/ and I always want to catch up / on my sleep.

③あと　私　起きる　/ とはいえ　/ 私　普段　好き　会うこと
After I wake up, / though, / I usually like to meet

/ 私の　友達　/ のために　1つの　素敵な　食事
/ my friends / for a nice meal

/ そして　1つの　長い　話。
/ and a long talk.

④に　日曜日　/ 私　ないだろう　寝る　/ あまりに　遅く。
On Sunday, / I wouldn't sleep / too late.

⑤私だろう　持つ　/1つの　素敵な　大きい　朝食
I'd have / a nice big breakfast

/何か ような パンケーキ。
/—something like pancakes.

⑥それから / 私だろう 見る 映画
Then / I'd watch movies

/ または 読む 1つの 面白い 本。
/ or read an interesting book.

⑦に 私 /これ だろう だ /1つの 完璧な 週末。
To me, / this would be / a perfect weekend.

❖ 覚えよう

B1 **How would you describe your perfect weekend?**

My perfect weekend would be sleeping at home all day on Saturday. This is because I am very busy during the week and I always want to catch up on my sleep. After I wake up, though, I usually like to meet my friends for a nice meal and a long talk. On Sunday, I wouldn't sleep too late. I'd have a nice big breakfast—something like pancakes. Then I'd watch movies or read an interesting book. To me, this would be a perfect weekend.

❖ 話してみよう

A1 What did you bring to school today?

A2 What do you think is the most useful thing you have with you now?

B1 Why did you choose to bring the things you have with you today?

15 Home Electronics
家電・機械

❖ **質問しよう**

A1 あなたは自宅にある炊飯器のブランドを覚えていますか。
Can you remember the brand of rice cooker you have at home?

A2 あなたの自宅にある電気製品は何ですか。
Could you name some home appliances that you have?

B1 自宅にある電気製品の中で最も便利なものを説明してください。
Would you describe the most useful appliance in your home?

❖ **答えよう**

A1 Can you remember the brand of rice cooker you have at home?
象印です。// タイガーだと思います。// 思い出せません。
Zojirushi. // Tiger, I think. // I can't remember.

A2 Could you name some home appliances that you have?
もちろん。うちにはエアコン、冷蔵庫、洗濯機、それから食洗機があります。
Sure. I have an air conditioner, a refrigerator, a washing machine, and a dishwasher.

B1 Would you describe the most useful appliance in your home?
①家にある最も便利な製品は食洗機と言わざるを得ません。
I'd have to say that the most useful appliance in my home is the dishwasher.

②私は毎日少なくとも１度はそれを使います。
I use it at least once every day.

15 **Home Electronics** 家電・機械

③私は本当に皿洗いが嫌いです。そのため、この製品を使うことでその家事を免れることができます。

I really dislike washing dishes, so this appliance lets me avoid that chore.

④また、食洗機を使うことでたくさん時間を節約できるので、家族と過ごす時間をさらに増やすことができます。

Also, using the dishwasher saves a lot of time, so I'm able to be with my family more.

❖ 練習しよう：❶ 単語ごとに英訳しよう
❷「／」ごとに英訳しよう

B1 Would you describe the most useful appliance in your home?

①私だろう　なければならない　言う
I'd have to say

／ということ　その　最も　役立つ　製品
/ that the most useful appliance

／に　私の　家　／だ　その　食洗機。
/ in my home / is the dishwasher.

②私　使う　それ　／少なくとも　／1回　毎日。
I use it / at least / once every day.

③私　本当に　嫌い　／洗うこと　皿
I really dislike / washing dishes,

／だから　／この　製品　させる　私　避ける　／その　雑用。
/ so / this appliance lets me avoid / that chore.

④また　／使うこと　その　食洗機　／セーブする　たくさんの　時間
Also, / using the dishwasher / saves a lot of time,

／だから　／私できる　だ　／と一緒に　私の　家族　より多い。
/ so / I'm able to be / with my family more.

15 Home Electronics 家電・機械

❖ 覚えよう

B1 Would you describe the most useful appliance in your home?

I'd have to say that the most useful appliance in my home is the dishwasher. I use it at least once every day. I really dislike washing dishes, so this appliance lets me avoid that chore. Also, using the dishwasher saves a lot of time, so I'm able to be with my family more.

❖ 話してみよう

A1 Do you like going to electronics stores?
A2 What would you like to buy at an electronics store?
B1 Do you think people depend on electronic devices too much? Why, or why not?

16 Housework
家事

❖ 質問しよう

> **A1** あなたは自分の部屋を掃除することが好きですか。
> Do you like cleaning your room?
>
> **A2** あなたはどのくらいの頻度で自分の部屋を掃除しますか。
> How often do you clean your room?
>
> **B1** 自分の部屋をどのように掃除するか詳しく説明してください。
> Could you explain in detail how you clean your room?

❖ 答えよう

A1 **Do you like cleaning your room?**
はい。// いいえ。// はい、好きです。// いいえ、好きではありません。
Yes. // No. // Yes, I do. // No, I don't.

A2 **How often do you clean your room?**
私は週1回掃除します。
I clean my room once a week.

B1 **Could you explain in detail how you clean your room?**
①まず最初に、私はベッドをきれいにします。
First of all, I make my bed.

②それから、自分の机とテーブルをきれいにし、そしてすべてを整理整頓します。
Then I clean up my desk and the table and organize everything.

③一番大きな仕事はすべての洋服を片づけることです。なぜなら平日は忙しく疲れているので、すべてをきれいにしておくことはできません。
The biggest job is putting away all my clothes because during the week, I'm too busy and tired to keep everything neat.

④私はそれを終えた後、部屋中に掃除機をかけます。普段それは、最後にします。

After I finish that, I vacuum the whole room, which is usually the last thing I do.

❖ 練習しよう：❶ 単語ごとに英訳しよう
　　　　　　　❷「 / 」ごとに英訳しよう

B1 Could you explain in detail how you clean your room?

①最初　の　すべて　/ 私　作る　私の　ベッド。
First of all, / I make my bed.

②それから　/ 私　きれいにする　私の　机　/ そして　その　テーブル
Then / I clean up my desk / and the table

/ そして　整理する　すべてのもの。
/ and organize everything.

③その　最も大きい　仕事　だ　/ 置くこと　離れて　すべて　私の　服
The biggest job is / putting away all my clothes

/ なぜなら　間　その　週　/ 私だ　あまりに　忙しい
/ because during the week, / I'm too busy

/ そして　疲れている　/ ため　保つ　すべてのもの　きちんと。
/ and tired / to keep everything neat.

④あと　私　終える　それ　/ 私　掃除機をかける　その　全体の　部屋
After I finish that, / I vacuum the whole room,

/ それ　だ　普段　/ その　最後の　こと　/ 私　する。
/ which is usually / the last thing / I do.

❖ 覚えよう

B1 **Could you explain in detail how you clean your room?**

First of all, I make my bed. Then I clean up my desk and the table and organize everything. The biggest job is putting away all my clothes because during the week I'm too busy and tired to keep everything neat. After I finish that, I vacuum the whole room, which is usually the last thing I do.

❖ 話してみよう

A1 Who does most of the housework in your home?

A2 How much time do you spend doing housework each week?

B1 Do you think married couples should share the housework? Why, or why not?

17 Parties
パーティー

❖ 質問しよう

A1 あなたはパーティーに行くことが好きですか。
Do you like going to parties?

A2 パーティーについて好きなことは何ですか。
What do you like about parties?

B1 あなたが参加したパーティーについて話してもらえませんか。
Could you describe a party you attended?

❖ 答えよう

A1 Do you like going to parties?
はい。// いいえ。// はい、好きです。// いいえ、好きではありません。// あまり。
Yes. // No. // Yes, I do. // No, I don't. // Not really.

A2 What do you like about parties?
私は人々と話したり笑ったりすることが好きです。
I like to talk and laugh with people.

B1 Could you describe a party you attended?
①私が今まで出席した中で最も印象的なパーティーは、私の大学の卒業パーティーでした。

The most impressive party I have ever attended was my university graduation party.

②みんな素敵なドレスやスーツで着飾っていました。

Everybody was dressed up in nice dresses and suits.

③私はみんなの姿や振る舞いを見て、大人になったと感じました。

I felt everyone had become adults because of the way they looked and acted.

④また、出された食事もとてもおいしかったです。
The food they offered was very nice, too.

⑤私は本当のそのパーティーを楽しみました。
I really enjoyed that party.

❖ 練習しよう:❶ 単語ごとに英訳しよう
❷「/」ごとに英訳しよう

B1 Could you describe a party you attended?

①その 最も 印象的な パーティー / 私 持つ 今までに 出席した
The most impressive party / I have ever attended

/ だった 私の 大学 卒業 パーティー。
/ was my university graduation party.

②みな だった 着飾る / に 素敵な ドレス そして スーツ。
Everybody was dressed up / in nice dresses and suits.

③私は 感じた / すべての人 持った なった 大人
I felt / everyone had become adults

/ のせいで その 方法 / 彼ら 見えた そして 振る舞った。
/ because of the way / they looked and acted.

④その 食べ物 / 彼ら 提供した / だった とても 素敵 も。
The food / they offered / was very nice, too.

⑤私 本当に 楽しんだ / その パーティー。
I really enjoyed / that party.

❖ 覚えよう

B1 Could you describe a party you attended?

The most impressive party I have ever attended was my university graduation party. Everybody was dressed up in nice dresses and suits. I felt everyone had become adults because of the way they looked and acted. The food they offered was very nice, too. I really enjoyed that party.

❖ 話してみよう

> **A1** Have you ever planned a party for a friend or family member?
>
> **A2** What kinds of parties are common in Japan?
>
> **B1** Based on movies or television, how do Japanese parties differ from parties in other countries?

18 Moving
引越し

❖ **質問しよう**

A1 今までに引越しをしたことがありますか。
Have you ever moved to a new house?

A2 新しい家に引越す時に最も難しいことは何ですか。
What is the most difficult thing about moving to a new house?

B1 どの地域に引越したいと思いますか。そして、それはなぜですか。
Which area would you most like to move to and why?

❖ **答えよう**

A1 Have you ever moved to a new house?
はい、10年前に。// はい。// いいえ。// はい、あります。// いいえ、ありません。
Yes, ten years ago. // Yes. // No. // Yes, I have. // No, I haven't.

A2 What is the most difficult thing about moving to a new house?
引越しで最も難しいことは、何を残して何を捨てるかを決めることです。
The most difficult thing about moving is deciding what things to keep and what to throw away.

B1 Which area would you most like to move to and why?
①私は沖縄に引越したいです。というのは、沖縄は温暖な気候で、人々が本当に優しいからです。
I would like to move to Okinawa because Okinawa has a mild climate and the people there are really nice.

②沖縄の人々は寿命が長いです。
Okinawans have long lifespans.

③これは、彼らが食べる食べ物と人生に対する姿勢によるものかもしれません。

This may be because of the food they eat or their attitude toward life.

④たとえ理由は何であっても、私がそこへ引越せば、今より長生きできるかもしれないと思います。

Whatever the reason is, I think I might be able to live longer if I move there.

❖ 練習しよう：❶ 単語ごとに英訳しよう
　　　　　　❷「 / 」ごとに英訳しよう

B1 Which area would you most like to move to and why?

①私は　たい　引越す　/ に　沖縄

I would like to move / to Okinawa

/ なぜなら　沖縄　持つ　1つの　温暖な　気候

/ because Okinawa has a mild climate

/ そして　その　人々　そこで　/ だ　本当に　素敵だ。

/ and the people there / are really nice.

②沖縄の人々　持つ　長い　寿命。

Okinawans have long lifespans.

③これは　かもしれない　だ　のせいで　その　食べ物 / 彼ら　食べる

This may be because of the food / they eat

/ または　彼らの　姿勢　に向かって　人生。

/ or their attitude toward life.

④たとえ〜でも　その　理由　だ　/ 私　思う

Whatever the reason is, / I think

/ 私　かもしれなかった　できる　生きる　より長く

/ I might be able to live longer

/ もし　私　引越す　そこへ。

/ if I move there.

❖ 覚えよう

B1 **Which area would you most like to move to and why?**

I would like to move to Okinawa because Okinawa has a mild climate and the people there are really nice. Okinawans have long lifespans. This may be because of the food they eat or their attitude toward life. Whatever the reason is, I think I might be able to live longer if I move there.

❖ 話してみよう

A1 Do you want to move to a new house or apartment?

A2 What are some important points to consider when choosing a moving company?

B1 Could you describe a strategy to ensure that everything goes smoothly when moving to a new house or apartment?

19 Procedures
手続き

❖ 質問しよう

A1 あなたは運転免許証を持っていますか。
Do you have a driver's license?

A2 パスポートの申請の仕方を教えてください。
How do you apply for a passport?

B1 大学での履修登録の手続きを教えてください。
Could you describe the procedure for registering for classes at a university?

❖ 答えよう

A1 Do you have a driver's license?
はい。// いいえ。// はい、持っています。// いいえ、持っていません。
Yes. // No. // Yes, I do. // No, I don't.

A2 How do you apply for a passport?
私は必要な書類を集めて、パスポート用の写真を撮ります。それから、それらを申請書と一緒にパスポート事務所の事務官に提出します。

I gather the necessary documents and get a passport photo. Then, I submit them with an application form to an official at the passport office.

B1 Could you describe the procedure for registering for classes at a university?

①最初に、履修登録手続きについての基本的な情報を教えてくれるオリエンテーションに参加します。

First, we attend an orientation that gives us basic information about the registration procedures.

②それから、インターネットで自分たちがとりたい授業を選びます。

Then, we go online and select the classes that we want to take.

③授業を選び終わったら、必要な情報をオンラインでただ提出するだけです。
When we've chosen our classes, we just submit the necessary information online.

④その後、大学から確認通知が届きます。
Later, we get confirmation from the university.

⑤これが、私の大学で履修登録をする手続きについての簡単な説明です。
This is a brief explanation of the procedure to register for classes at my university.

❖ 練習しよう：❶ 単語ごとに英訳しよう
　　　　　　　❷「／」ごとに英訳しよう

B1 Could you describe the procedure for registering for classes at a university?

①最初に ／私たち 出席する １つの オリエンテーション
First, / we attend an orientation

／それ 与える 私たち 基本的な 情報
/ that gives us basic information

／について その 登録 手続。
/ about the registration procedures.

②それから 私たち 行く オンライン
Then, we go online

／そして セレクトする その 授業
/ and select the classes

／それ 私たち ほしい とること。
/ that we want to take.

③時 私たち持つ 選んだ 私たちの 授業
When we've chosen our classes,

／私たち ちょうど 提出する ／その 必要な 情報 ／オンラインで。
/ we just submit / the necessary information / online.

④後で ／私たち 得る 確認 から その 大学。
Later, / we get confirmation from the university.

⑤これ　だ　１つの　簡単な　説明　/の　その　手続き
This is a brief explanation of the procedure

/ため　登録する　のため　授業　/で　私の　大学。
/ to register for classes / at my university.

❖ 覚えよう

B1 **Could you describe the procedure for registering for classes at a university?**

First, we attend an orientation that gives us basic information about the registration procedures. Then, we go online and select the classes that we want to take. When we've chosen our classes, we just submit the necessary information online. Later, we get confirmation from the university. This is a brief explanation of the procedure to register for classes at my university.

❖ 話してみよう

A1 Is it easy to get a library card?

A2 What kind of information do you need to provide to get a cell phone?

B1 Can you describe the process of getting a driver's license in your country?

20 Love
恋愛

❖ 質問しよう

A1 あなたはロマンチックな映画が好きですか。
Do you like romantic movies?

A2 東京で人気のあるデートスポットはどこですか。
What are some popular dating spots in Tokyo?

B1 あなたの国の典型的なデートについて教えてください。
Could you describe a typical date in your country?

❖ 答えよう

A1 Do you like romantic movies?
はい。// いいえ。// はい、好きです。// いいえ、好きではありません。// あまり。
Yes. // No. // Yes, I do. // No, I don't. // Not really. // Not so much.

A2 What are some popular dating spots in Tokyo?
私はお台場のようなウォーターフロントか、渋谷や新宿のようなショッピング・スポットが、デートに人気なスポットだと思います。
I think waterside areas, such as Odaiba, or shopping spots, like Shibuya and Shinjuku, are popular for dating.

B1 Could you describe a typical date in your country?
①私たちはたいてい駅で待ち合わせます。
We usually meet at a train station.
②それから一緒にショッピングに行くか映画を見ます。
Then we go shopping together or watch a movie.
③そのあと、たいてい素敵なレストランに夕食に行きます。
After that, we usually go for dinner at a nice restaurant.

④これが私の国の典型的なデートです。
 This is a typical date in my country.
⑤また、ディズニーランドに行くのもカップルにはとても人気があります。
 Also, going to Disneyland is very popular for couples.
⑥そこで一日中一緒に過ごすことができます。
 It's easy to spend the whole day together there.

❖ 練習しよう：❶ 単語ごとに英訳しよう
　　　　　❷「 / 」ごとに英訳しよう

B1 Could you describe a typical date in your country?

①私たち　普段　会う　/ で　1つの　列車　駅。
 We usually meet / at a train station.
②それから　私たち　行く　ショッピング　一緒に
 Then / we go shopping together

 / または　見る　1つの　映画。
 / or watch a movie.
③あと　それ　/ 私たち　普段　行く　のため　夕食
 After that, / we usually go for dinner

 / で　1つの　素敵な　レストラン。
 / at a nice restaurant.
④これ　だ　1つの　典型的な　デート　/ の　私の　国。
 This is a typical date / in my country.
⑤また　/ 行くこと　に　ディズニーランド　/ だ　とても　一般的
 Also, / going to Disneyland / is very popular

 / にとって　カップル。
 / for couples.
⑥それだ　簡単　/ 費やすこと　その　全部の　日　/ 一緒に　そこで。
 It's easy / to spend the whole day / together there.

❖ 覚えよう

B1 **Could you describe a typical date in your country?**

We usually meet at a train station. Then we go shopping together or watch a movie. After that, we usually go for dinner at a nice restaurant. This is a typical date in my country. Also, going to Disneyland is very popular for couples. It's easy to spend the whole day together there.

❖ 話してみよう

A1 Is it a good idea to use an internet dating service to find a boyfriend or girlfriend?

A2 What are some common ways that people meet boyfriends or girlfriends in your country?

B1 What are the good points and bad points of using an internet dating service to find a partner?

21 Marriage
結婚

❖ 質問しよう

A1 今までに結婚式に行ったことがありますか。
Have you ever been to a wedding?

A2 結婚適齢期はいつだと思いますか。
What is the best age to get married?

B1 結婚生活を長持ちさせる秘訣を教えてください。
What is the secret to having a long marriage?

❖ 答えよう

A1 Have you ever been to a wedding?
はい。// いいえ。// はい、あります。// いいえ、ありません。// いとこの結婚式です。

Yes. // No. // Yes, I have. // No, I haven't. // My cousin's wedding.

A2 What is the best age to get married?
それは本当に人によると思います。// 結婚適齢期は30歳ぐらいだと思います。

It really depends on the person. // I think the best age to get married is around thirty.

B1 What is the secret to having a long marriage?
①それは答えるのに難しい質問です。

That's a difficult question to answer.

②でも、私の両親を思うと、彼らは長い間結婚しています。私はお互いに尊敬の念を見せることが、結婚生活を成功させる鍵だと思います。

But if I think about my parents, who have been married for a long time, I can say that showing respect to each other is the key to a successful marriage.

③彼らはお互いを思いやり、そして直面しているいかなる問題についていつも話し合いをします、だから、よくコミュニケーションをとることもまたとても重要だと言えます。
They treat each other well, and they always talk about any problems they're having, so I'd say good communication is also very important.

❖ 練習しよう：❶ 単語ごとに英訳しよう
　　　　　　❷「/」ごとに英訳しよう

B1 What is the secret to having a long marriage?

①それだ　1つの　難しい　質問　/ため　答える。
That's a difficult question / to answer

②しかし　/もし　私　考える　について　私の　両親
But / if I think about my parents,

/彼ら　持つ　だった　結婚した　/間　1つの　長い　時間
/ who have been married / for a long time,

/私　できる　言う　/ということ　見せること　尊敬　に　お互い
/ I can say / that showing respect to each other

/だ　その　鍵　/に　1つの　成功的な　結婚。
/ is the key / to a successful marriage.

③彼ら　扱う　お互い　よく　/そして　彼ら　いつも　話す
They treat each other well, / and they always talk

/について　あらゆる　問題　/彼らだ　持っている
/ about any problems / they're having,

/だから　/私だろう　言う　/よい　コミュニケーション　だ
/ so / I'd say / good communication is

/また　とても　重要。
/ also very important.

21 Marriage 結婚

❖ 覚えよう

B1 What is the secret to having a long marriage?

That's a difficult question to answer. But if I think about my parents, who have been married for a long time, I can say that showing respect to each other is the key to a successful marriage. They treat each other well, and they always talk about any problems they're having, so I'd say good communication is also very important.

❖ 話してみよう

A1 Would you like to work as a wedding planner?
A2 Who are some famous married couples in your country?
B1 Could you describe the ideal marriage?

22 Childbirth & Childcare
出産・育児

❖ **質問しよう**

> **A1** あなたはどこで生まれましたか。
> Where were you born?
>
> **A2** あなたは幼いころどんなことをするのが好きでしたか。
> What did you like to do when you were a little child?
>
> **B1** どうしたらいい親になれますか。
> What makes a good parent?

❖ **答えよう**

A1 Where were you born?
名古屋です。// 青森です。// 東京の病院です。
Nagoya. // In Aomori. // At a hospital in Tokyo.

A2 What did you like to do when you were a little child?
私は車の図鑑を見ることと車のおもちゃで遊ぶことが好きでした。
I liked to look at photo books of cars and play with toy cars.

B1 What makes a good parent?
①いい親でいるためには、勇気づけと忍耐が必要です。
Being a good parent requires encouragement and patience.

②子供たちに、スポーツや楽器のような何か新しいことや難しいことへの挑戦を促すことなど、勇気づけには多くの種類があります。
Encouragement can take many forms, including urging our children to attempt something new or difficult, like a sport or a musical instrument.

③あるいは、子供たちが自転車乗りなどに最初に失敗した時でも、勇気づけは、子供たちをもう一度トライさせることに導いていきます
Or it might be guiding them to try something again, like riding a bicycle, if they fail at first.

④我々は子供たちの変化をすぐには見ることができないかもしれないので、忍耐は重要です。

Patience is important because we may not see immediate changes in our children.

⑤しかしながら、子供たちが新しいことにトライする間、一貫して勇気づけを与えること、そして、忍耐強くあることによって、我々は子供たちの成長を助けることができるのです。

However, by offering consistent encouragement and then being patient while they try new things, we can help our children flourish.

❖ 練習しよう：❶ 単語ごとに英訳しよう
　　　　　　 ❷「／」ごとに英訳しよう

B1 What makes a good parent?

①であること　1つの　良い　親　/ 要求する　勇気づけ　/ そして　忍耐。

Being a good parent / requires encouragement / and patience.

②勇気づけ　できる　とる　多くの　形　/ 含んでいる

Encouragement can take many forms, / including

／促すこと　我々の　子供たち　/ 試みること　何か　新しい

/ urging our children / to attempt something new

／や　難しい　／ような　1つの　スポーツ　／や　1つの　音楽の　楽器。

/ or difficult, / like a sport / or a musical instrument.

③または、/ それ　かもしれなかった　である　導いている　彼ら

Or / it might be guiding them

／トライすること　何か　再び　／ような　乗ること　1つの　自転車

/ to try something again, / like riding a bicycle,

／もし　彼ら　失敗する　最初に。

/ if they fail at first.

④忍耐　である　重要　／なぜなら　我々　かもしれない　ない　見る

Patience is important / because we may not see

／すぐの　変化　／に　我々の　子供たち。

/ immediate changes / in our children.

⑤しかしながら　/によって　提供すること　一貫した　勇気づけ
However, / by offering consistent encouragement

/そして　それから　/であること　我慢強い　/間　彼ら　トライする
/ and then / being patient / while they try

/新しい　こと　/我々　できる　助ける　/我々の　子供たち　開花する。
/ new things, / we can help / our children flourish.

❖ 覚えよう

B1 What makes a good parent?

Being a good parent requires encouragement and patience. Encouragement can take many forms, including urging our children to attempt something new or difficult, like a sport or a musical instrument. Or it might be guiding them to try something again, like riding a bicycle, if they fail at first. Patience is important because we may not see immediate changes in our children. However, by offering consistent encouragement and then being patient while they try new things, we can help our children flourish.

❖ 話してみよう

A1 Where were you born?
A2 What is the ideal age for a mother to give birth to a child?
B1 What do children need in order to be happy and healthy?

23 Memories
思い出

❖ 質問しよう

> **A1** 5歳以前の子供時代の出来事で覚えていることがありますか。
> Can you remember anything from your childhood before the age of five?
>
> **A2** あなたの一番古い思い出は何ですか。
> What is your earliest memory?
>
> **B1** あなたが中学・高校生だったころの好きな思い出を教えてください。
> Could you describe a favorite memory from when you were a middle school student?

❖ 答えよう

A1 **Can you remember anything from your childhood before the age of five?**

はい。// いいえ。// はい、思い出せます。// いいえ、思い出せません。// いくつか。

Yes. // No. // Yes, I can. // No, I can't. // A few things.

A2 **What is your earliest memory?**

私の最も古い思い出は、幼稚園のブランコに乗っていたことです。

My earliest memory is riding a swing in kindergarten.

B1 **Could you describe a favorite memory from when you were a middle school student?**

①中学・高校時代の私の大好きな思い出はクラブに参加していたことです。

My favorite memory from middle school is participating in my club activities.

②私はバレーボール部の部員でした。

I was a member of the volleyball club.

③私たちは、毎日とてもハードに練習しました。
We practiced very hard every day.

④私たちのチームはあまり強くはありませんでしたが、チームワークがとてもよかったです。
Even though our team was not so strong, we had good teamwork.

⑤これが私の中高時代の大好きな思い出です。
This is my favorite memory from middle school.

⑥実際、私はそのクラブのたくさんの人とまだよい友達でいます。
In fact, I'm still good friends with a lot of people from that club.

❖ 練習しよう：❶ 単語ごとに英訳しよう
　　　　　　❷「／」ごとに英訳しよう

B1 **Could you describe a favorite memory from when you were a middle school student?**

①私の　好きな　思い出　／から　中等　学校
My favorite memory / from middle school

／だ　参加すること　に　私の　クラブ　活動。
/ is participating in my club activities.

②私　だった　1つの　メンバー　／の　その　バレーボール　クラブ。
I was a member / of the volleyball club.

③私たち　練習した　とても　ハードに　／毎日。
We practiced very hard / every day.

④たとえ～ても　／私たちの　チーム　だった　ない　それほど　強い
Even though / our team was not so strong,

／私たち　持った　よい　チームワーク。
/ we had good teamwork.

⑤これ　だ　私の　好きな　思い出　／から　中等　高校。
This is my favorite memory / from middle school.

⑥実際 / 私だ　まだ　よい　友達 / と一緒に　たくさんの　人々
In fact, / I'm still good friends / with a lot of people

/ から　そのクラブ。
/ from that club.

❖ 覚えよう

B1 **Could you describe a favorite memory from when you were a middle school student?**

My favorite memory from middle school is participating in my club activities. I was a member of the volleyball club. We practiced very hard every day. Even though our team was not so strong, we had good teamwork. This is my favorite memory from middle school. In fact, I'm still good friends with a lot of people from that club.

❖ 話してみよう

> **A1** Do you have a good memory?
>
> **A2** What kinds of experiences and events do people tend to remember?
>
> **B1** If you had to choose between keeping a diary or taking photographs, which would you choose and why?

24 Dreams & Goals
夢・目標

❖ 質問しよう

A1 あなたには将来のはっきりとした計画がありますか。
Do you have a clear plan for your future?

A2 子供のころどんな職業に就きたいと思っていましたか。
What kind of job did you want when you were a child?

B1 あなたの夢を実現するための最善の方法は何ですか。
What is the best way to achieve your dreams?

❖ 答えよう

A1 **Do you have a clear plan for your future?**
はい。// いいえ。// はい、あります。// いいえ、ありません。// あまり。
Yes. // No. // Yes, I do. // No, I don't. // Not really.

A2 **What kind of job did you want when you were a child?**
私は子供のころ、フライト・アテンダントになりたかったです。
I wanted to become a flight attendant when I was a child.

B1 **What is the best way to achieve your dreams?**
①私は最善の方法は夢を見続けることだと思います。
I think the best way is to continue dreaming.
②私たちはあきらめるべきではありません。
We should not give up.
③こうするためには、夢を自分の近くに置いておくことです。
To do this, it's important to keep your dream close to you.

④例えば、もし、あなたがプロサッカー選手になりたいのだとしたら、毎日練習することはもちろん必要ですが、サッカーについての本を読んだり、サッカー選手の写真を自分の部屋に置いたりというようなこともすべきです。

For example, if you want to be a professional soccer player, you need to play every day of course, but you should also read books about soccer, have pictures of soccer players in your room and things like that.

⑤夢を常に忘れずにいることで、それを本当に実現できる道を見つけることができるかもしれません。

Keeping the dream alive puts us on the pathway to really making it happen.

❖ 練習しよう：❶ 単語ごとに英訳しよう
　　　　　　❷「 / 」ごとに英訳しよう

B1 What is the best way to achieve your dreams?

①私　思う　/その　ベストの　方法　だ　/続けること　夢見ること。
I think / the best way is / to continue dreaming.

②私たち　べき　ない　あきらめる。
We should not give up.

③ため　する　これ　/それだ　重要　/キープすること　あなたの　夢
To do this, / it's important / to keep your dream

/近くに　あなた。
/ close to you.

④例えば　/もし　あなた　ほしい　であること
For example, / if you want to be

/1つの　プロフェッショナル　サッカー　選手
/ a professional soccer player,

/あなた　必要だ　練習すること　毎日
/ you need to play every day

/もちろん　/しかし　/あなた　べき　また　読む　本
/ of course, / but / you should also read books

/について サッカー /持つ 写真 の サッカー 選手
/ about soccer, / have pictures of soccer players

/に あなたの 部屋 /そして もの ような それ。
/ in your room / and things like that.

⑤キープすること その 夢 生きている
Keeping the dream alive

/置く 私たち に その 道筋
/ puts us on the pathway

/に 本当に させること それ 起こる。
/ to really making it happen.

❖ 覚えよう

B1 **What is the best way to achieve your dreams?**

I think the best way is to continue dreaming. We should not give up. To do this, it's important to keep your dream close to you. For example, if you want to be a professional soccer player, you need to play every day of course, but you should also read books about soccer, have pictures of soccer players in your room and things like that. Keeping the dream alive puts us on the pathway to really making it happen.

❖ 話してみよう

A1 Do you want to be famous in the future?

A2 What do you do every day to move toward your future dreams?

B1 Could you explain the difference between dreams and goals?

25 Worries
悩み

❖ 質問しよう

> **A1** 今までに友達から何か相談を受けたことがありますか。
> Has a friend ever talked to you about a problem?
>
> **A2** 何か悩みがある時、あなたはどうしますか。
> What do you do when you're worried about something?
>
> **B1** 卒業後の就職先を見つけることで悩んでいる友達にあなたは何と言いますか。
> What would you tell a friend who is worried about finding a job after graduation?

❖ 答えよう

A1 **Has a friend ever talked to you about a problem?**
はい。// いいえ。// もちろん。// 何度も。
Yes. // No. // Of course. // Many times.

A2 **What do you do when you're worried about something?**
私は普段自分の悩みについて友達や家族と話します。
I usually try to share my worries with my friends or my family.

B1 **What would you tell a friend who is worried about finding a job after graduation?**

①私はいつも彼らの悩みを理解しようと努力し、そして仕事を探し続けるように励まします。

I always try to share their worries and encourage them to keep on looking for a job.

②私は「私たちにとってフルタイムの仕事を探すのは初めてなんだから、当然だよ。正直に言って私も少し不安だよ」というようなことを言うかもしれません。

I might say something like, "It's very natural for us to be worried since it's our first experience to look for a full-time job. To be honest, I'm a little worried, too."

③友達からの励ましは本当に私たちの不安を乗り越える助けになります。というのは、自分1人ではない、他の人たちも同じ気持ちなんだということをわからせてくれるからです。

Encouragement from friends really helps us overcome our worries since it gives us the feeling that we are not alone and that other people have the same feelings.

❖ 練習しよう：❶ 単語ごとに英訳しよう
　　　　　　❷「 / 」ごとに英訳しよう

B1 What would you tell a friend who is worried about finding a job after graduation?

①私　いつも　トライする　/シェアすること　彼らの　悩み

I always try / to share their worries

/そして　励ます　彼ら　/キープすること　探すこと　1つの　仕事。

/ and encourage them / to keep on looking for a job.

②私　かもしれなかった　言う　/何か　ような

I might say / something like,

/それだ　とても　自然　にとって　私たち　/心配すること

/ "It's very natural for us / to be worried

/ので　それだ　私たちの　最初の　経験

/ since it's our first experience

/探すこと　1つの　フルタイムの　仕事

/ to look for a full-time job.

正直に言うと　/私だ　少し　心配している　も。

To be honest, / I'm a little worried, too."

③励まし　から　友達　/本当に　助ける　私たち

Encouragement from friends / really helps us

/ 乗り越える　私たちの　悩み
/ overcome our worries

/ ので　それ　与える　私たち　その　感情
/ since it gives us the feeling

/ という　私たち　だ　ない　1人で
/ that we are not alone

/ そして　という　他の　人々　/ 持つ　その　同じ　感情。
/ and that other people / have the same feelings.

❖ 覚えよう

B1 **What would you tell a friend who is worried about finding a job after graduation?**

I always try to share their worries and encourage them to keep on looking for a job. I might say something like, "It's very natural for us to be worried since it's our first experience to look for a full-time job. To be honest, I'm a little worried, too." Encouragement from friends really helps us overcome our worries since it gives us the feeling that we are not alone and that other people have the same feelings.

❖ 話してみよう

> **A1** Have you ever worried about an exam?
> **A2** What are some things that university students worry about?
> **B1** Could you describe an effective way to reduce stress?

26 Death
死

❖ 質問しよう

A1 あなたは死後の世界を信じますか。
Do you believe in life after death?

A2 人が亡くなると、その人の魂はどこに行くと思いますか。
When a person dies, where do you think his or her spirit goes?

B1 日本の典型的なお葬式について話してください。
Could you describe a typical Japanese funeral?

❖ 答えよう

A1 Do you believe in life after death?
はい。// いいえ。// はい、信じています。// いいえ、信じていません。// よくわかりません。
Yes. // No. // Yes, I do. // No, I don't. // I'm not sure.

A2 When a person dies, where do you think his or her spirit goes?
私は私たちの魂は死後最愛の家族の心の中に生き続けると思います。
I think after death, our souls will stay in the hearts of our loved ones.

B1 Could you describe a typical Japanese funeral?
①典型的な日本のお葬式は２つの儀式から成り立ちます。
The typical funeral in Japan consists of two ceremonies.

②１つはお通夜と呼ばれるものです。
One is called *otsuya*.

③私たちはこの儀式を火葬の前日に行います。
We hold this ceremony the night before the cremation.

④人々は亡くなった方と亡くなった方の家族に祈りを捧げるためにこの儀式に参加します。
People come to the ceremony to pray for the person who passed away and for his or her family.

⑤それから、火葬の日には、告別式と呼ばれる儀式を行い、そこで人々はその亡くなった方を火葬に送り出します。
Then, on the day of the cremation, we have a ceremony called *kokubetsu shiki*, where people send the person who passed away to be cremated.

⑥しかしながら、最近、日本のこのお葬式の習慣も変わりつつあります。
However, recently the funeral customs in Japan have been changing, too.

❖ 練習しよう：❶ 単語ごとに英訳しよう
　　　　　　　❷「 / 」ごとに英訳しよう

B1 Could you describe a typical Japanese funeral?

①その　典型的な　葬式　に　日本
The typical funeral in Japan

/構成される　から　2つ　セレモニー。
/ consists of two ceremonies.

②1つ　だ　呼ばれる　お通夜。
One is called *otsuya*.

③私たち　持つ　この　セレモニー　/その　夜　前　その　火葬。
We hold this ceremony / the night before the cremation.

④人々　来る　に　その　セレモニー　/ため　祈る　のため　その　人
People come to the ceremony / to pray for the person

/その人　亡くなった
/ who passed away

/そして　のため　彼の　または　彼女の　家族。
/and for his or her family.

⑤それから　/に　その　日　の　その　火葬
Then, / on the day of the cremation,

/私たち 持つ 1つの セレモニー /呼ばれる 告別式
/ we have a ceremony / called *kokubetsu shiki*,

/そこで 人々 送る その 人 /その人 亡くなった
/ where people send the person / who passed away

/ため だ 火葬される。
/ to be cremated.

⑥しかしながら /最近 /その 葬式 習慣 に 日本
However, / recently / the funeral customs in Japan

/持つ だった 変わっている も。
/ have been changing, too.

❖ 覚えよう

B1 **Could you describe a typical Japanese funeral?**

The typical funeral in Japan consists of two ceremonies. One is called *otsuya*. We hold this ceremony the night before the cremation. People come to the ceremony to pray for the person who passed away and for his or her family. Then, on the day of the cremation, we have a ceremony called *kokubetsu shiki*, where people send the person who passed away to be cremated. However, recently the funeral customs in Japan have been changing, too.

❖ 話してみよう

A1 Do you think animals feel sad when another one dies?

A2 What are some things you can do to have a longer life?

B1 Could you explain a typical Buddhist or Shinto view of death?

27 Family
家族

❖ **質問しよう**

> **A1** あなたは何人家族ですか。
> How many people are there in your family?
>
> **A2** あなたの家族の誰かについて話してください。
> Could you describe someone in your family?
>
> **B1** あなたが家族と一緒に過ごした休暇について話してください。
> Could you describe a vacation you've taken with your family?

❖ **答えよう**

A1 How many people are there in your family?
3人です。// 5人です。
Three. // Five people.

A2 Could you describe someone in your family?
私の姉はとても思いやりがあり面倒みがよく、そして彼女はいつも私をよりうまくいくように励ましてくれます。
My older sister is very thoughtful and caring, and she always encourages me to do better.

B1 Could you describe a vacation you've taken with your family?
①家族と一緒に取った最も印象的な休暇は、沖縄への旅でした。
The most impressive vacation that I've taken with my family was a trip to Okinawa.

②海の近くの小さなホテルに泊まって、1週間過ごしました。
We stayed at a small hotel by the ocean and spent a week there.

③毎日泳ぎに行ったり魚釣りに行ったりしました。
We went swimming and fishing every day.

④またバーベキューもしました。
We had barbeques together, too.

⑤それが、家族と一緒に過ごした一番の旅行でした。
It was a great trip with my family.

❖ 練習しよう：❶ 単語ごとに英訳しよう
   ❷「 / 」ごとに英訳しよう

B1 Could you describe a vacation you've taken with your family?

①その　最も　印象的な　休暇　/ それ　私持つ　とった
The most impressive vacation / that I've taken

/ と一緒に　私の　家族　/ だった　1つの　旅　に　沖縄。
/ with my family / was a trip to Okinawa.

②私たち　滞在した　に　1つの　小さい　ホテル　/ そば　その　海
We stayed at a small hotel / by the ocean

/ そして　費やした　1週間　そこで。
/ and spent a week there.

③私たち　行った　泳ぐこと　/ そして　魚釣り　毎日。
We went swimming / and fishing every day.

④私たち　持った　バーベキュー　一緒に　も。
We had barbeques together, too.

⑤それ　だった　1つの　偉大な　旅　/ と一緒に　私の　家族。
It was a great trip / with my family.

❖ 覚えよう

B1 **Could you describe a vacation you've taken with your family?**

The most impressive vacation that I've taken with my family was a trip to Okinawa. We stayed at a small hotel by the ocean and spent a week there. We went swimming and fishing every day. We had barbeques together, too. It was a great trip with my family.

❖ 話してみよう

A1 Do you have any brothers or sisters?

A2 Could you talk about a happy memory you have of your family?

B1 Could you describe the good points and bad points of having a very large family?

28 Friendship
友達

❖ 質問しよう

> **A1** あなたの親友の1人の名前を教えてください。
> Could you tell me the name of one of your good friends?
>
> **A2** 高校時代の親友について話をしてください。
> Could you describe a good friend from high school?
>
> **B1** あなたの友達について何か面白い話を教えてください。
> Would you tell a funny story about one of your friends?

❖ 答えよう

A1 **Could you tell me the name of one of your good friends?**
歌子です。

Utako.

A2 **Could you describe a good friend from high school?**
歌子は頭がよくて勤勉でそして思いやりがあります。私たちは高校時代にはいつも一緒でした。

Utako is smart, diligent and thoughtful. We were inseparable in high school.

B1 **Would you tell a funny story about one of your friends?**
①私の友達の1人の歌子はいつも私たちを笑わせてくれました。

One of my friends, Utako, always tried to make us laugh.

②彼女は有名女優や歌手の真似がとても上手でした。

She was very good at imitating famous actresses or singers.

③私たちがつるんでいた時はいつでも、彼女は有名人のような話し方をして、私たちを笑わせてくれました。

Whenever we hung out together, she would always try to talk like a celebrity, and that made us laugh.

④彼女はあまりにも人の真似が上手なので、私は彼女の本当の性格がわかりませんでした。

She was so good at imitating people that I couldn't tell what her real personality was like.

❖ 練習しよう：❶ 単語ごとに英訳しよう
　　　　　　❷「/」ごとに英訳しよう

B1 Would you tell a funny story about one of your friends?

①1人　の　私の　友達　/ 歌子 / いつも　トライする

One of my friends, / Utako, / always tried

/ させること　私たち　笑う。

/ to make us laugh.

②彼女　だった　とても　上手　真似すること

She was very good at imitating

/ 有名な　女優　または　歌手。

/ famous actresses or singers.

③いつでも　私たち　遊んだ　一緒に

Whenever we hung out together,

/ 彼女　〜たものだ　いつも　トライする

/ she would always try

/ 話すこと　/ ように　1つの　有名人

to talk / like a celebrity,

/ そして　それ　させた　私たち　笑う。

/ and that made us laugh.

④彼女　だった　そんなに　上手　真似すること　人々

She was so good at imitating people

/ なので　私　できなかった　言う

/ that I couldn't tell

/ 何　彼女の　本当の　性格　だった　ような。

/ what her real personality was like.

❖ 覚えよう

B1 **Would you tell a funny story about one of your friends?**

One of my friends, Utako, always tried to make us laugh. She was very good at imitating famous actresses or singers. Whenever we hung out together, she would always try to talk like a celebrity, and that made us laugh. She was so good at imitating people that I couldn't tell what her real personality was like.

❖ 話してみよう

> **A1** How do you say "friend" in your language?
> **A2** What is a good way to make new friends?
> **B1** What is your definition of a true friend?

29 Personality
性格

❖ 質問しよう

> **A1** 真面目な性格の人とのんきな性格の人と、あなたはどちらとうまくやっていけますか。
>
> Do you get along better with people who are serious or easygoing?
>
> **A2** あなた自身の性格を説明してください。
>
> How would you describe your own personality?
>
> **B1** どんな性格の人がリーダーに適しているかを話してください。
>
> Could you tell me what kind of personality is suitable for a leader?

❖ 答えよう

A1 **Do you get along better with people who are serious or easygoing?**

真面目な人です。// のんきな人です。

Serious people. // Easygoing.

A2 **How would you describe your own personality?**

私はかなりのんきです。私は本当に物事にくよくよしません。

I am quite easygoing. I don't really worry about things.

B1 **Could you tell me what kind of personality is suitable for a leader?**

①私は、リーダーは責任感、決断力があり、そして信頼できる人であるべきだと思います。

I think a leader should be responsible, decisive and trustworthy.

②リーダーが責任感と決断力を持つべき理由は、とても素早く、難しくそして公平な決断をしなくてはいけない場面があるからです。特に人々の意見が異なる時はなおさらです。

The reason the leader should be responsible and decisive is that there are situations where he or she has to make a difficult and fair decision very quickly—especially when people have different opinions.

③リーダーは自分の部下全員が躊躇なくアドバイスを求められるように、信頼が厚い人でなければなりません。

The leader has to be trustworthy so that everybody under him or her can ask for advice without hesitation.

❖ 練習しよう：❶ 単語ごとに英訳しよう
❷「／」ごとに英訳しよう

B1 Could you tell me what kind of personality is suitable for a leader?

① 私 思う ／1つの リーダー べき だ 責任感がある ／決断力がある
I think / a leader should be responsible, / decisive

／そして 信頼できる。
／ and trustworthy.

② その 理由 ／その リーダー べき だ 責任感がある
The reason / the leader should be responsible

／そして 決断力がある ／だ ということ ／そこにある 場面
/ and decisive / is that / there are situations

／そこで 彼 または 彼女 なければならない 作ること
/ where he or she has to make

／1つの 難しい そして 公平な 決断 ／とても 素早く
/ a difficult and fair decision / very quickly

／特に ／時 人々 もつ ／異なる 意見。
/ —especially / when people have / different opinions.

③ その リーダー なければならない だ 信頼できる
The leader has to be trustworthy

／～ように ／みな の下 彼 または 彼女
/ so that / everybody under him or her

/できる 求める アドバイス /なしに 躊躇。
/ can ask for advice / without hesitation.

❖ 覚えよう

B1 **Could you tell me what kind of personality is suitable for a leader?**

I think a leader should be responsible, decisive and trustworthy. The reason the leader should be responsible and decisive is that there are situations where he or she has to make a difficult and fair decision very quickly—especially when people have different opinions. The leader has to be trustworthy so that everybody under him or her can ask for advice without hesitation.

❖ 話してみよう

A1 Can you summarize your personality in one or two words?
A2 What kind of people do you get along with best?
B1 What can a person do if she doesn't like her personality?

30 Feelings
感情

❖ 質問しよう

> **A1** あなたは笑うことが好きですか。
> Do you like to laugh?
>
> **A2** あなたはどんなことで笑いますか。
> What makes you laugh?
>
> **B1** あなたに起きたことで何か面白い話をしてください。
> Could you describe something funny that happened to you?

❖ 答えよう

A1 Do you like to laugh?

はい。// はい、好きです。// もちろんです。

Yes. // Yes, I do. // Of course.

A2 What makes you laugh?

いつも私を笑わせてくれるテレビに出てくるコメディアンが何人かいます。

There are some comedians on TV that always make me laugh.

B1 Could you describe something funny that happened to you?

①ある日、私が間違って姉の携帯電話を手にしたら、誰かから電話がかかってきました。

I took my sister's cellphone by mistake one day and got a phone call from someone.

②相手は私の姉のボーイフレンドでした。

It was my sister's boyfriend.

③彼は私が姉だと思い込んで、そしてデートに誘いました。

He thought I was my sister, and he started asking me to go out.

④彼があまりにも速く話すので、途中で遮って、彼が間違った人と話をしていることを知らせることができませんでした。だから私はあきらめて姉のためにデートの約束をしました。

He talked so fast that I couldn't interrupt and let him know he was talking to the wrong person, so I gave up and made a date for my sister!

❖ 練習しよう：❶ 単語ごとに英訳しよう
　　　　　　❷「/」ごとに英訳しよう

B1 Could you describe something funny that happened to you?

①私　とる　私の　姉の　携帯電話　/間違って　ある日
I took my sister's cellphone / by mistake one day
/そして　得た　1つの　電話　コール　/から　誰か。
/ and got a phone call / from someone.

②それ　だった　私の　姉の　ボーイフレンド。
It was my sister's boyfriend.

③彼　思った　/私　だった　私の　姉
He thought / I was my sister,
/そして　彼　スタートした　尋ねること　私　/外出すること。
/ and he started asking me / to go out.

④彼　話した　そんなに　速く　/なので　私　できなかった　遮る
He talked so fast / that I couldn't interrupt
/そして　させる　彼　知る　/彼　だった　話している
/ and let him know / he was talking
/に　その　間違った　人　/だから　私　あきらめた
/ to the wrong person, / so / I gave up
/そして　作った　1つの　デート　のため　私の　姉。
/ and made a date for my sister!

❖ 覚えよう

B1 **Could you describe something funny that happened to you?**

I took my sister's cellphone by mistake one day and got a phone call from someone. It was my sister's boyfriend. He thought I was my sister, and he started asking me to go out. He talked so fast that I couldn't interrupt and let him know he was talking to the wrong person, so I gave up and made a date for my sister!

❖ 話してみよう

A1 Do you feel happy right now?

A2 What can you do to make yourself happy when you feel sad?

B1 How does food affect a person's mood?

31 Appearance
容姿

❖ 質問しよう

> **A1** あなたはお母さんに似ていますか。
> Do you look like your mother?
>
> **A2** あなたの親友の容姿を描写してください。
> Could you describe your best friend's appearance?
>
> **B1** その人の外見からわかる性格について何か話してください。
> What can you tell about someone's personality based on his or her appearance?

❖ 答えよう

A1 **Do you look like your mother?**
はい。// いいえ。// はい、似ています。// いいえ、似ていません。// いいえ、あまり。// 少し。
Yes. // No. // Yes, I do. // No, I don't. // Not really. // A little.

A2 **Could you describe your best friend's appearance?**
私の親友は髪が長くて背が高いです。
My best friend has long hair and is very tall.

B1 **What can you tell about someone's personality based on his or her appearance?**

①えー、2人の男性がいると思ってください。
Well, imagine that there are two men.

②1人は長髪で、ひげを伸ばし 両耳にイヤリングをしています。
One has long hair, a beard, and earrings in both ears.

③もう1人は髪は短くさっぱりしています。
The other man has short, neat hair.

④彼はメガネをしてスーツを着ています。
　He's wearing glasses and a suit.

⑤どちらの人が、より真面目で、緊張していると思うかと尋ねれば、たいていは、髪の短い人を選ぶと思います。
　If I asked which person looks more serious and uptight, I think most people would choose the guy with the short hair.

⑥より自由で、型にはまらないのが誰かを尋ねれば、たいていの人々は長髪の人を選ぶことは間違いありません。
　And if I asked who looks more free-spirited and unconventional, I'm sure most people would choose the man with the long hair.

❖ 練習しよう：❶ 単語ごとに英訳しよう
　　　　　　　❷「／」ごとに英訳しよう

B1 What can you tell about someone's personality based on his or her appearance?

①えー　想像しなさい　／ということ　そこにいる　２人の　男性。
　Well, imagine / that there are two men.

②１人　持つ　長い　髪　／１つの　ひげ　／そして　イヤリング
　One has long hair, / a beard, / and earrings

／に　両方の　耳。
／ in both ears.

③その　他の　男性　／持つ　短い　きちんとした　髪。
　The other man / has short, neat hair.

④彼だ　着ている　メガネ　／そして　１つの　スーツ。
　He's wearing glasses / and a suit.

⑤もし　私　尋ねた　／どちらの　人　見える　より　真面目
　If I asked / which person looks more serious

／そして　緊張している　／私　思う　／ほとんどの　人々　だろう　選ぶ
／ and uptight, / I think / most people would choose

／その　男　と一緒の　その　短い　髪。
／ the guy with the short hair.

⑥そして　もし　私　尋ねた　/誰　見える　より　自由な気質
And if I asked / who looks more free-spirited

/そして　型にはまらない
/ and unconventional,

/私だ　確か　/ほとんどの　人々　だろう　選ぶ
/ I'm sure / most people would choose

/その　男　と一緒の　その　長い　髪。
/ the man with the long hair.

❖ 覚えよう

B1 **What can you tell about someone's personality based on his or her appearance?**

Well, imagine that there are two men. One has long hair, a beard, and earrings in both ears. The other man has short, neat hair. He's wearing glasses and a suit. If I asked which person looks more serious and uptight, I think most people would choose the guy with the short hair. And if I asked who looks more free-spirited and unconventional, I'm sure most people would choose the man with the long hair.

❖ 話してみよう

A1 Do you check your appearance in the mirror every day?

A2 How important is a person's appearance when applying for a job?

B1 What advice would you give to a friend who didn't like her appearance?

32 Personal Relationships
人づきあい

❖ 質問しよう

A1 あなたはたいていの人とはうまくやっていけますか。
Do you get along well with most people?

A2 もしレストランで働いていて、お客さんがあなたに何度かとても失礼な話し方をしたら、あなたはどうしますか。
What would you do if you were working in a restaurant and a customer spoke very rudely to you several times?

B1 人とうまくやっていくための秘訣を教えてください。
What is the best way to get along well with people?

❖ 答えよう

A1 Do you get along well with most people?
はい。// はい、やっていけます。// そう思います。// いいえ、あまり。
Yes. // Yes, I do. // I think so. // Not really.

A2 What would you do if you were working in a restaurant and a customer spoke very rudely to you several times?
それは、答えるのが難しい質問ですね。でも、そのお客さんに自分の失礼さを認識してもらえるように、私はそのお客に対してさらに丁寧に話しかけると思います。
It's very difficult to answer this question, but I would start speaking to the customer more politely, hoping he would recognize his own rudeness.

B1 What is the best way to get along well with people?
①私は正直であることと、他人に対して心を広げておくことが最も重要なことだと思います。
I think the most important thing is to try to be honest and to open our minds to other people.

②またユーモアも重要だと思います。
   I also think humor is important.
③私は普段相手と打ち解ける方法として、何か失礼のない冗談を言う機会を見つけるようにしています。
   I usually try to find a chance to make a polite joke as a way to break the ice.
④正直さとユーモアがあれば、人は私を信頼でき、私と過ごす時間が楽しいものであるとわかってくれると思います。
   With honesty and humor, I think people will see that they can trust me and that it's fun to spend time with me.

❖ 練習しよう：❶ 単語ごとに英訳しよう
❷「／」ごとに英訳しよう

B1 What is the best way to get along well with people?

①私　思う　／その　最も　重要な　こと　だ
  I think / the most important thing is

  ／トライすること　であること　正直
  / to try to be honest

  ／そして　開くこと　私たちの　心　／に　他の　人々。
  / and to open our minds / to other people.

②私　また　思う　／ユーモア　だ　重要。
  I also think / humor is important.

③私　普段　トライする　見つけること　／1つの　機会　ため　作る
  I usually try to find / a chance to make

  ／1つの　丁寧な　ジョーク　／として　1つの　方法
  / a polite joke / as a way

  ／ため　壊す　その　氷。
  / to break the ice.

④と一緒に　正直さ　そして　ユーモア　／私　思う
  With honesty and humor, / I think

/ 人々　だろう　見る　/ ということ　彼ら　できる　信頼する　私
/ people will see / that they can trust me

/ そして　ということ　それだ　楽しみ　/ 過ごすこと　時間
/ and that it's fun / to spend time

/ と一緒に　私。
/ with me.

❖ 覚えよう

B1 What is the best way to get along well with people?

I think the most important thing is to try to be honest and to open our minds to other people. I also think humor is important. I usually try to find a chance to make a polite joke as a way to break the ice. With honesty and humor, I think people will see that they can trust me and that it's fun to spend time with me.

❖ 話してみよう

A1 Do you like meeting new people?

A2 When you meet a new person, what kinds of topics do you usually talk about?

B1 How important are personal relationships when searching for a job?

33 Disagreements & Arguments
喧嘩・トラブル

❖ 質問しよう

A1 友達と深刻な意見の対立をしたことがありますか。
Have you ever had a serious disagreement with a friend?

A2 一般的な口論の内容は何でしょうか。
What are some common causes of arguments?

B1 深刻な口論をした後、友達と仲直りをする最善の方法は何ですか。
What is the best way to make up with a friend after a serious argument?

❖ 答えよう

A1 **Have you ever had a serious disagreement with a friend?**
はい。// いいえ。// はい、あります。// 一度もありません。// もちろん。
Yes. // No. // Yes, I have. // Never. // Sure.

A2 **What are some common causes of arguments?**
単純な誤解が多くの口論の原因です。
Many arguments are caused by simple misunderstandings.

B1 **What is the best way to make up with a friend after a serious argument?**

①おかげさまで、私は友達とあまり口論したことがありません。でも、もし口論したら、私は謝るためにメールを送ると思います。
Thankfully, I haven't had many arguments with my friends, but if I did have one, I guess I'd send an email to apologize.

②そして、それから、一緒に出かける計画をします。
And then I'd try to make a plan to go out together.

③それで、相手と会う時には、会ってできるだけ早い段階で面と向かって謝ります。
Then, when we were together I'd apologize face-to-face as

33 Disagreements & Arguments 喧嘩・トラブル

soon as we met.

④もし私が悪いと感じていたら、彼あるいは彼女に夕食をおごります。
If I felt I was wrong, I'd try to buy him or her dinner.

⑤これが友達と仲直りするよい方法です。
This would be a good way to make up with a friend.

❖ 練習しよう：❶ 単語ごとに英訳しよう
　　　　　　 ❷「／」ごとに英訳しよう

B1 What is the best way to make up with a friend after a serious argument?

①おかげさまで ／私 持たない 持った 多くの 口論
Thankfully, / I haven't had many arguments

／と一緒に 私の 友達 ／しかし ／もし 私 した 持つ １つ
/ with my friends, / but / if I did have one,

／私 推測する ／私だろう 送る １つの Eメール ため 謝る。
/ I guess / I'd send an email to apologize.

②そして それから ／私だろう トライする 作ること １つの プラン
And then / I'd try to make a plan

／ため 出かける 一緒に。
/ to go out together.

③それから ／時 私たち だった 一緒に ／私だろう 謝る
Then, / when we were together / I'd apologize

／面と向かって ／できるだけ早く 私たち 会った。
/ face-to-face / as soon as we met.

④もし 私 感じた 私 だった 間違い
If I felt I was wrong,

／私だろう トライする 買うこと 彼 または 彼女 夕食。
/ I'd try to buy him or her dinner.

⑤これ だろう だ １つの いい 方法
This would be a good way

/ ため　仲直りする　と一緒に　1人の　友達。
/ to make up with a friend.

❖ 覚えよう

B1 **What is the best way to make up with a friend after a serious argument?**

Thankfully, I haven't had many arguments with my friends, but if I did have one, I guess I'd send an email to apologize. And then I'd try to make a plan to go out together. Then, when we were together I'd apologize face-to-face as soon as we met. If I felt I was wrong, I'd try to buy him or her dinner. This would be a good way to make up with a friend.

❖ 話してみよう

> **A1** Do you think it is natural to have arguments with other people?
>
> **A2** What is the best way to respond to someone who wants to argue with you?
>
> **B1** In what ways can arguments be helpful?

34 Customs & Manners
マナー・習慣

❖ 質問しよう

A1 今まで友人の家に招待されたことがありますか。

Have you ever been invited to a friend's house?

A2 日本では、誰かの家に上がる時、どうしますか。

In Japan, what do you usually do when you enter someone's house?

B1 日本人家庭にホームステイする外国人留学生に何かアドバイスをしてください。

What advice would you give to a foreign student who is going to do a homestay with a Japanese family?

❖ 答えよう

A1 Have you ever been invited to a friend's house?

はい。// いいえ。// はい、あります。// 何度も。// 1度も。

Yes. // No. // Yes, I have. // Many times. // Never.

A2 In Japan, what do you usually do when you enter someone's house?

私たちは普段靴を脱ぎます。

We usually take off our shoes.

B1 What advice would you give to a foreign student who is going to do a homestay with a Japanese family?

①最初に覚えておかなければならないことは、日本の家に入る時には靴を脱ぐことです。

The first thing you need to remember is to take off your shoes when entering a Japanese home.

②それはとても重要です。

It's very important.

34 Customs & Manners マナー・習慣

③ことわざにあるように、郷に入れば郷に従いなさい。
As the saying goes, "When in Rome…."

④日本の生活を体験するためにホームステイしているということを忘れるべきではありません。
You should not forget that you're doing a homestay to get a taste of Japanese life.

⑤あなたは新しい経験を楽しむべきだと思います。
I mean you should enjoy the new experiences.

⑥例えば、たとえ奇妙に見えても、ホストファミリーから出された食べ物はすべて食べてみるべきだと思います。
For example, you should try every kind of food the host family offers, even if it seems strange.

❖ 練習しよう：❶ 単語ごとに英訳しよう
　　　　　　❷「 / 」ごとに英訳しよう

B1 What advice would you give to a foreign student who is going to do a homestay with a Japanese family?

①その　最初の　こと　/あなた　必要だ　覚えておくこと　だ
The first thing / you need to remember is

/脱ぐこと　あなたの　靴　/時　入ること　1つの　日本の　家。
/ to take off your shoes / when entering a Japanese home.

②それだ　とても　重要。
It's very important.

③ように　その　格言　行く　/時　に　ローマ
As the saying goes, / "When in Rome…."

④あなた　べき　ない　忘れる　/ということ　あなただ　している
You should not forget / that you're doing

/1つの　ホームステイ　/ため　得る　ちょっとした　日本の　生活。
/ a homestay / to get a taste of Japanese life.

⑤私は　意味する　/あなた　べき　楽しむ　/その　新しい　経験。
I mean / you should enjoy / the new experiences.

⑥例えば　/あなた　べき　トライする　/すべての　種類　の　食べ物
For example, / you should try / every kind of food
/その　ホストファミリー　提供する
/ the host family offers,
/たとえ〜ても　/それ　ようだ　変わっている。
/ even if / it seems strange.

❖ 覚えよう

B1 What advice would you give to a foreign student who is going to do a homestay with a Japanese family?

The first thing you need to remember is to take off your shoes when entering a Japanese home. It's very important. As the saying goes, "When in Rome…." You should not forget that you're doing a homestay to get a taste of Japanese life. I mean you should enjoy the new experiences. For example, you should try every kind of food the host family offers, even if it seems strange.

❖ 話してみよう

> A1 Do you think it is important to have good manners?
> A2 What are some examples of bad manners you've seen?
> B1 How should parents teach good manners to their children?

35 Schools
学校（小・中・高等学校）

❖ 質問しよう

> **A1** あなたはどこで小学校へ通っていましたか。
> Where did you go to elementary school?
>
> **A2** あなたの小学校で一番気に入っていたことは何ですか。
> What did you like best about your elementary school?
>
> **B1** あなたの好きな小学校の先生について話してください。
> Would you tell me about your favorite elementary school teacher?

❖ 答えよう

A1 Where did you go to elementary school?
横浜です。// 東京都内です。
Yokohama. // In Tokyo.

A2 What did you like best about your elementary school?
私は友達と一緒に給食を食べることが本当に好きでした。その学校の給食がかなり美味しかったです。
I really liked eating lunch with my friends. The school lunches were pretty good.

B1 Would you tell me about your favorite elementary school teacher?

① 4年生の担任の先生が好きでした。
My fourth grade teacher was my favorite.

② 先生はかなり年をとっていましたが、とてもエネルギッシュでした。
He was quite old but very energetic.

③ 例えば、先生は、休憩時間はいつも私たちと遊んでくれました。
For example, he always played with us during recess.

④私たちは 放課後にも、かくれんぼうや野球のようなことをしました。
We played hide-and-seek, baseball and things like that after school, too.
⑤クラスでは、先生の過去についての面白い話を、よく私たちにしてくれました。
In class, he often told us interesting stories about his past.
⑥私たちは先生ととても楽しく過ごしました。
We had a lot of fun with him.

❖ 練習しよう：❶ 単語ごとに英訳しよう
　　　　　　　❷「 / 」ごとに英訳しよう

B1 Would you tell me about your favorite elementary school teacher?

①私の 4番目の 学年 先生 / だった 私の お気に入り。
My fourth grade teacher / was my favorite.

②彼 だった かなり 年をとっている
He was quite old

/ しかし とても エネルギッシュ。
/ but very energetic.

③例えば / 彼 いつも 遊んだ と一緒に 私たち / 間 休憩。
For example, / he always played with us / during recess.

④私たち 遊んだ かくれんぼう / 野球 / そして こと ような その
We played hide-and-seek, / baseball / and things like that.

/ 後で 学校 も。
/ after school, too.

⑤に クラス / 彼 よく 話した 私たち / 面白い 話
In class, / he often told us / interesting stories

/ について 彼の 過去。
/ about his past.

⑥私たち 持った たくさんの 楽しさ / と一緒に 彼。
We had a lot of fun / with him.

❖ 覚えよう

B1 **Would you tell me about your favorite elementary school teacher?**

My fourth grade teacher was my favorite. He was quite old but very energetic. For example, he always played with us during recess. We played hide-and-seek, baseball and things like that after school, too. In class, he often told us interesting stories about his past. We had a lot of fun with him.

❖ 話してみよう

> **A1** Did you wear a uniform at your high school?
>
> **A2** What is one good point of wearing a uniform to school?
>
> **B1** What are the disadvantages of not wearing a school uniform?

36 University
学校（大学）

❖ **質問しよう**

> **A1** あなたの専攻は何ですか。
> What's your major?
>
> **A2** どのくらいの間あなたが選んだ専攻に興味を持っていますか。
> How long have you been interested in the major you chose?
>
> **B1** なぜあなたの専攻を選んだのですか。
> Why did you choose your major?

❖ **答えよう**

A1 **What's your major?**

英文学です。// 美術史です。// 社会学です。

English literature. // Art history. // Sociology.

A2 **How long have you been interested in the major you chose?**

私は中学生の時からずっと英語に興味を持っています。

I have been interested in English since I was in junior high school.

B1 **Why did you choose your major?**

①えー、私の専攻は英語です。

Well, my major is English.

②私は将来英語の先生になることに興味があるので、この専攻を選びました。

I chose this major because I'm interested in becoming an English teacher in the future.

③私はずっと教えることがしたくて、また私は本当に英語が好きなので、それは私にとって完璧な選択だと思っています。

I have always wanted to teach, and I really like English, so it seemed like the perfect choice for me.

④私は英語と教え方の両方をたくさん学んでいます。

I'm learning a lot about both English and teaching.

⑤私は私の専攻がよい先生になるために必要な技術を与えてくれることを願っています。

I hope that my major will give me the skills I will need to be an effective teacher.

❖ 練習しよう：❶ 単語ごとに英訳しよう　❷「／」ごとに英訳しよう

B1 Why did you choose your major?

①えー ／ 私の 専攻 だ 英語。
Well, / my major is English.

②私 選んだ この 専攻 ／ なぜなら 私だ 興味がある
I chose this major / because I'm interested

／ に なること 1つの 英語 教師 ／ に その 未来。
/ in becoming an English teacher / in the future.

③私は 持つ いつも ほしかった 教えること
I have always wanted to teach,

／そして 私 本当に 好きだ 英語
/ and I really like English,

／だから それ ようだった ように その 完全な 選択
/ so it seemed / like the perfect choice

／にとって 私。
/ for me.

④／ 私だ 学んでいる たくさん ／ について 両方 英語
I'm learning a lot / about both English

/ そして　教えること。
/ and teaching.

⑤私　望む
I hope

/ ということ　私の　専攻　だろう　与える　私　その　スキル
/ that my major will give me the skills

/ 私　だろう　必要だ　/ ため　だ　1つの　効果的な　教師。
/ I will need / to be an effective teacher.

❖ 覚えよう

B1 **Why did you choose your major?**

Well, my major is English. I chose this major because I'm interested in becoming an English teacher in the future. I have always wanted to teach, and I really like English, so it seemed like the perfect choice for me. I'm learning a lot about both English and teaching. I hope that my major will give me the skills I will need to be an effective teacher.

❖ 話してみよう

> **A1** Are you a good student?
> **A2** Could you tell me about your study habits?
> **B1** What advice would you give to a student starting at university next year?

37 Grades
成績

❖ 質問しよう

> **A1** あなたは高校時代の成績に満足でしたか。
> Were you satisfied with your high school grades?
>
> **A2** 高校時代あなたは普段週にどのくらいの時間勉強しましたか。
> How many hours a week did you usually study in high school?
>
> **B1** あまり一生懸命頑張らなくてもよい成績がとれる方法を教えてください。
> Could you tell me how to get good grades without working too hard?

❖ 答えよう

A1 Were you satisfied with your high school grades?
はい。// いいえ。// はい、満足でした。// いいえ、満足ではありませんでした。// あまり。
Yes. // No. // Yes, I was. // No, I wasn't. // Not really.

A2 How many hours a week did you usually study in high school?
私は2年生までは1日約1時間勉強しました。でも3年生になって、私は大学入学試験の準備をするために1日約4時間勉強しました。
I studied about one hour a day until my second year. But when I became a senior, I studied about four hours a day to prepare for my university entrance exams.

B1 Could you tell me how to get good grades without working too hard?
①それは答えるのが難しい質問です。
That's a tough question.

②でも私が言えることは、一歩一歩勉強することは重要だということです。
But what I can say is that it's important to study step-by-step.
③試験前に詰め込む代わりに、私たちは毎日たとえ短い時間でもよいので、勉強する習慣を作るべきです。そうすれば毎日学習したことを復習できます。
Instead of cramming before an exam, we should make a habit of studying every day—even for a short time— so that we can review what we learn each day.
④これによって学んだことをより覚えることができます。
This allows us to better remember what we learn.
⑤私はこの方法で成績がよくなりました。
This is how I improved my grades.

❖ 練習しよう：❶ 単語ごとに英訳しよう
　　　　　　　 ❷「 / 」ごとに英訳しよう

B1 Could you tell me how to get good grades without working too hard?

①それだ　1つの　タフな　質問。
That's a tough question.
②しかし　/ 何　私　できる　言う　だ　/ ということ　それだ　重要
But / what I can say is / that it's important

/ 勉強すること　一歩一歩。
/ to study step-by-step.
③代わりに　の　詰め込むこと　/ 前に　1つの　試験
Instead of cramming / before an exam,

/ 私たち　べき　作る　1つの　癖　/ の　勉強すること　毎日
/ we should make a habit / of studying every day

/ たとえ　間　1つの　短い　時間
/ —even for a short time—

/ 〜ように　/ 私たち　できる　復習する
/ so that / we can review

/ 何　私たち　学ぶ　それぞれの　日。
/ what we learn each day.

④これ　許す　私たち　/こと　よりよく　覚える　/何　私たち　学ぶ。
This allows us / to better remember / what we learn.

⑤これ　だ　/どのように　私　改善した　/私の　成績。
This is / how I improved / my grades.

❖ 覚えよう

B1 **Could you tell me how to get good grades without working too hard?**

That's a tough question. But what I can say is that it's important to study step-by-step. Instead of cramming before an exam, we should make a habit of studying every day—even for a short time—so that we can review what we learn each day. This allows us to better remember what we do in class. This is how I improved my grades.

❖ 話してみよう

> **A1** On a scale of one to ten, how important is getting good grades?
>
> **A2** How can university students get good grades?
>
> **B1** How important is your GPA (grade point average) in finding a good job?

38 Tests
試験

❖ 質問しよう

> **A1** 今までに TOEIC を受けたことがありますか。
> Have you ever taken the TOEIC?
>
> **A2** 今まで受けた中で最も難しかったテストは何ですか。
> What is the most difficult test you've ever taken?
>
> **B1** テストの上手な攻略法を教えてください。
> Could you describe some good test-taking strategies?

❖ 答えよう

A1 **Have you ever taken the TOEIC?**
はい。// いいえ。// はい、あります。// いいえ、ありません。
Yes. // No. // Yes, I have. // No, I haven't.

A2 **What is the most difficult test you've ever taken?**
私が今まで受けた中で最も難しかったテストは高校入試の数学の問題です。
The most difficult test I have ever taken is the math section of my high school entrance exam.

B1 **Could you describe some good test-taking strategies?**
①えー、難しいテストを生き抜くための鍵は、うまく時間を管理することです。
Well, good time management is the key to surviving a difficult test, I think.

②私はテストを受け取ったら、どの質問に最初に答えて、どの質問を最後に解くかを見極めるために、まず全体をざっと見ます。
First of all, when I get the test, I take a look at the whole thing to decide which question I should answer first and which I should answer last.

③それからケアレスミスがないかどうかを確認できるように、全部の質問にテスト終了の 10 分前には答え終わるように努力します。
Then I try to finish answering all the questions about ten minutes before the end so that I can make sure there are no careless mistakes.

④もしそれが数学のテストであれば、検算をします。
If it is a math test, I check the calculations again.

❖ 練習しよう：❶ 単語ごとに英訳しよう
　　　　　❷「 / 」ごとに英訳しよう

B1 Could you describe some good test-taking strategies?

①えー ／よい 時間 管理 ／だ その 鍵
Well, / good time management / is the key

／に サバイバルするため 1つの 難しい テスト ／私 思う。
/ to surviving a difficult test, / I think.

②最初 の すべて ／時 私 得る その テスト
First of all, / when I get the test,

／私 ざっと見る その すべての もの ／ため 決める
/ I take a look at the whole thing / to decide

／どの 質問 私 べき 答える 最初に
/ which question I should answer first

／そして どれ 私 べき 答える 最後に。
/ and which I should answer last.

③それから ／私 トライする 終えること 答えること
Then / I try to finish answering

／すべての その 質問 ／だいたい 10分 前に その 終わり
/ all the questions / about ten minutes before the end

／〜ように ／私 できる 作る 確かだ
/ so that / I can make sure

／そこにある ない ケアレスミス。
/ there are no careless mistakes.

④もし それ だ 1つの 数学 テスト
If it is a math test,

／私 チェックする その 計算 再び。
／I check the calculations again.

❖ 覚えよう

B1 **Could you describe some good test-taking strategies?**

Well, good time management is the key to surviving a difficult test, I think. First of all, when I get the test, I take a look at the whole thing to decide which question I should answer first and which I should answer last. Then I try to finish answering all the questions about ten minutes before the end so that I can make sure there are no careless mistakes. If it is a math test, I check the calculations again.

❖ 話してみよう

A1 Do you usually study before a test?

A2 What do you usually do on the day before an important test?

B1 What should schools do to prevent cheating on exams?

39 Extracurricular Activities
課外活動

❖ 質問しよう

> **A1** もう大学のサークルには入りましたか。
> Have you joined any clubs at your university yet?
>
> **A2** 高校時代に最も人気のあった部活は何でしたか。
> What was the most popular club or team at your high school?
>
> **B1** クラブに所属するメリットは何ですか。
> What are some of the benefits of belonging to a club?

❖ 答えよう

A1 **Have you joined any clubs at your university yet?**
はい。// いいえ。// はい、入りました。// いいえ、入っていません。// まだです。// ラクロスクラブです。

Yes. // No. // Yes, I have. // No, I haven't. // Not yet. // The lacrosse club.

A2 **What was the most popular club or team at your high school?**
男子の間で最も人気があったのは野球部で、女子の間で人気があったのは吹奏楽部でした。

The baseball team was the most popular for boys, and the school band was the most popular among girls.

B1 **What are some of the benefits of belonging to a club?**
①クラブに参加することの1つのメリットはチームワークを学べることです。

One of the benefits of participating in a club is that we can learn about good teamwork.

②あるクラブの一員である時、他人とうまくやっていくことは必須のことです。
Getting along with other people is essential when you are a member of a club.

③2番目は、普段の教室では学べない技能を学べることです。
Secondly, we can learn skills that we can't learn in classrooms.

④例えば、ギタークラブに参加すれば、ギターが弾けるようになりますが、この技能は普通の授業では教えてもらえません。
For example, if we belong to a guitar club, we can learn how to play the guitar, a skill that isn't offered in regular classes.

⑤私はクラブ活動から学ぶことはたくさんあると思います。
I think we can learn a lot from club activities.

❖ 練習しよう：❶ 単語ごとに英訳しよう
　　　　　　❷「／」ごとに英訳しよう

B1 What are some of the benefits of belonging to a club?

① 1つ の その 利点 ／の 参加すること に 1つの クラブ
One of the benefits / of participating in a club

／だ ということ ／私たち できる 学ぶ
/ is that / we can learn

／について よい チームワーク。
/ about good teamwork.

②と仲良くやっていく 他の 人々 ／だ 必須
Getting along with other people / is essential

／時 あなた だ 1つの メンバー ／の 1つの クラブ。
/ when you are a member / of a club.

③2つめに ／私たち できる 学ぶ スキル
Secondly, / we can learn skills

／それ 私たち できない 学ぶ ／に 教室。
/ that we can't learn / in classrooms.

④例えば / もし 私たち 所属する に 1つの ギタークラブ
For example, / if we belong to a guitar club,

/私たち できる 学ぶ /仕方 演奏する その ギター
/ we can learn / how to play the guitar,

/1つの スキル /それ でない 提供される /に 通常の 授業。
/ a skill / that isn't offered / in regular classes.

⑤私 思う / 私たち できる 学ぶ たくさん /から クラブ活動。
I think / we can learn a lot / from club activities.

❖ 覚えよう

B1 **What are some of the benefits of belonging to a club?**

One of the benefits of participating in a club is that we can learn about good teamwork. Getting along with other people is essential when you are a member of a club. Secondly, we can learn skills that we can't learn in classrooms. For example, if we belong to a guitar club, we can learn how to play the guitar, a skill that isn't offered in regular classes. I think we can learn a lot from club activities.

❖ 話してみよう

> **A1** Do most university students join clubs?
>
> **A2** How much time do university students spend on club activities each week?
>
> **B1** What are some reasons university students choose not to join clubs?

40 Research & Development
調査・研究

❖ 質問しよう

A1 もう大学の図書館は利用しましたか。
Have you used the university library yet?

A2 卒業論文を書くことについてあなたはどう思いますか。
What are your thoughts on writing a graduation thesis?

B1 あなたの専門に関連した重要な理論について話してください。
Could you describe an important theory related to your major?

❖ 答えよう

A1 Have you used the university library yet?
はい。// いいえ。// はい、利用しました。// まだです。
Yes. // No. // Yes, I have. // Not yet.

A2 What are your thoughts on writing a graduation thesis?
それはとても大変そうです。私は常にそれに取り組んで、定期的に論文のアドバイザーに会わなければいけないと思います。
It seems so tough. I imagine that I'll have to work on it constantly and meet my thesis advisor regularly.

B1 Could you describe an important theory related to your major?
①私は第2言語習得を学んでいて、最近先生がジェスチャーの使用が未知語の学習や記憶にいかに役立つか話してくれました。
I'm studying about second language acquisition, and recently my professor talked about how using gestures can help us learn and remember new vocabulary words.

②バイリンガルの子供が モノリンガルの子供よりもどのようにして多く ジェスチャーを使うかという記事も読みました。

We also read an article that showed how bilingual children use more gestures than monolingual children.

③それが私に当てはまるかどうかわからないので、いくつかのドイツ語の未知語のそれぞれに独特なジェスチャーを付けて学習してみて、それが私の記憶を強化するかどうか試すつもりです。

I'm not sure if it's true or not for me, so I'm trying to learn some new German vocabulary words with unique gestures for each one to see if it reinforces my memory.

❖ 練習しよう：❶ 単語ごとに英訳しよう
❷「／」ごとに英訳しよう

B1 Could you describe an important theory related to your major?

①私だ　勉強している　／について　第２言語習得

I'm studying / about second language acquisition,

／そして　最近　／私の　教授　話した

/ and recently / my professor talked

／について　どのように　使うこと　ジェスチャー

/ about how using gestures

／できる　助ける　私たち　学ぶ　／そして　覚える　新しい　語彙。

/ can help us learn / and remember new vocabulary words.

②私たち　また　読んだ　１つの　記事　／それ　見せた

We also read an article / that showed

／どのように　バイリンガルの　子供たち　使う

/ how bilingual children use

／より多くの　ジェスチャー　／よりも　モノリンガルの　子供たち。

/ more gestures / than monolingual children.

③私だ　ない　確か　／もし　それだ　本当　または　ない

I'm not sure / if it's true or not

/にとって 私 /だから /私だ トライしている 学ぶこと
/ for me, / so / I'm trying to learn

/いくつかの 新しい ドイツ語の 語彙
/ some new German vocabulary words

/と一緒に 独特な ジェスチャー /のため それぞれの 1つ
/ with unique gestures / for each one

/ため 見る もし それ 強化する 私の 記憶。
/ to see if it reinforces my memory.

❖ 覚えよう

B1 **Could you describe an important theory related to your major?**

I'm studying about second language acquisition, and recently my professor talked about how using gestures can help us learn and remember new vocabulary words. We also read an article that showed how bilingual children use more gestures than monolingual children. I'm not sure if it's true or not for me, so I'm trying to learn some new German vocabulary words with unique gestures for each one to see if it reinforces my memory.

❖ 話してみよう

> **A1** Have you ever written a research paper?
> **A2** What are some difficult points about conducting research?
> **B1** Could you explain a topic you learned about in one of your classes?

41 Music
音楽

❖ 質問しよう

> **A1** あなたはどんな音楽が好きですか。
> What kind of music do you like?
>
> **A2** あなたはいつ音楽を普段聞きますか。
> When do you usually listen to music?
>
> **B1** どんな音楽を聴くか、あなたはどうやって決めますか。
> How do you decide what music to listen to?

❖ 答えよう

A1 **What kind of music do you like?**
ジャズです。// Jポップです。// クラシックです。
Jazz. // J-pop. // Classical music.

A2 **When do you usually listen to music?**
私は登校途中に、特に電車の中で音楽を聴きます。
I usually listen to music on the way to school, especially on the train.

B1 **How do you decide what music to listen to?**
①私は自分の気分によって音楽を選びます。
I choose music according to my mood.

②例えば、少しストレスを感じている時は、ゆっくりとしたリラックスできる音楽を選びます。
For example, if I feel a little stressed, I choose slow and relaxing music.

③もし少し元気がほしい時は、気分を盛り上げるために、好きなロック音楽を選びます。
If I feel like I need some energy, I choose my favorite rock music to pick me up.

④もし集中しなくてはならない時は、何か軽い音楽を低音量で聞きます。
If I need to concentrate on something, I play some light music at low volume.

⑤もう1度言いますが、それは（どんな音楽をかけるかは）、すべて自分が置かれている状況と気分で決めます。
Again, it all depends on the situation I am in and my mood at the time.

❖ 練習しよう：❶ 単語ごとに英訳しよう
　　　　　　❷「／」ごとに英訳しよう

B1 How do you decide what music to listen to?

①私　選ぶ　音楽　/によって　私の　ムード。
I choose music / according to my mood.

②例えば　/もし　私　感じる　少し　ストレスされている
For example, / if I feel a little stressed,

/私　選ぶ　スローな　/そして　リラックスできる　音楽。
/ I choose slow / and relaxing music.

③もし　私　感じる　ように　/私　必要だ　いくらかの　エネルギー
If I feel like / I need some energy,

/私　選ぶ　私の　好きな　ロックミュージック
/ I choose my favorite rock music

/ため　拾う　私　上に。
/ to pick me up.

④もし　私　必要だ　集中すること　に　何か
If I need to concentrate on something,

/私　かける　いくつかの　軽い　音楽　/で　低い　音量。
/ I play some light music / at low volume.

⑤再び　/それ　すべて　依る　に　その　状況　/私　だ　に
Again, / it all depends on the situation / I am in

/そして　私の　ムード　/で　その　時。
/ and my mood / at the time.

❖ 覚えよう

B1 How do you decide what music to listen to?

I choose music according to my mood. For example, if I feel a little stressed, I choose slow and relaxing music. If I feel like I need some energy, I choose my favorite rock music to pick me up. If I need to concentrate on something, I play some light music at low volume. Again, it all depends on the situation I am in and my mood at the time.

❖ 話してみよう

> **A1** Do you play a musical instrument?
> **A2** How do you find out about new music?
> **B1** Why do people listen to music?

42 Visual Art
絵画

❖ 質問しよう

> **A1** 今までにとても印象に残る絵を見たことがありますか。
> Have you ever seen a very impressive painting?
>
> **A2** 絵を見るのに最適な場所はどこですか。
> Where's a good place to see paintings?
>
> **B1** 今までに描いた絵の中で一番上手に描けた絵を説明してください。
> Could you describe the best picture you've ever drawn?

❖ 答えよう

A1 **Have you ever seen a very impressive painting?**

はい。// いいえ。// はい、あります。// いいえ、ありません。

Yes. // No. // Yes, I have. // No, I haven't.

A2 **Where's a good place to see paintings?**

たくさん異なる種類の絵を見ることができるので、私は美術館が絵を見るのに最適な場所だと思います。

I think an art museum is a good place to see paintings because we can see many different kinds.

B1 **Could you describe the best picture you've ever drawn?**

①私はかつて小学生のころ私の先生の絵を描きました。

I once drew a picture of my teacher when I was in elementary school.

②その絵は、先生が満面の笑みを浮かべながらクラスで教えている絵でした。

My picture showed him teaching our class with a big smile on his face.

③私はかつて講読していた子供新聞にその絵を送りました。

I sent the picture to a newspaper for children that I used to read.

④その新聞は時々絵を掲載していました。

They sometimes posted pictures.

⑤驚いたことに、ある日新聞を開くと、私の先生の笑顔がありました。

To my surprise, one day I opened the newspaper, and there was my teacher's smiling face.

⑥それは私の絵だったのです。

It was my picture!

⑦私はその絵がとても自慢で、先生もそう思ってくれています。

I was very proud of it, and so was my teacher.

❖ 練習しよう：❶ 単語ごとに英訳しよう　❷「／」ごとに英訳しよう

B1 Could you describe the best picture you've ever drawn?

①私　かつて　描いた　1つの　絵　／の　私の　先生

I once drew a picture / of my teacher

／時　私　だった　に　小学校。

/ when I was in elementary school.

②私の　絵　見せた　彼　／教えている　我々の　クラス

My picture showed him / teaching our class

／と一緒に　1つの　大きな　微笑み　／上に　彼の　顔。

/ with a big smile / on his face.

③私　送った　その　絵　／に　1つの　新聞　のため　子供たち

I sent the picture / to a newspaper for children

／それ　私　していた　読む。

/ that I used to read.

④彼ら　時々　掲載した　絵。

They sometimes posted pictures.

⑤驚いたことに ／ある日 ／私 開いた その 新聞
To my surprise, / one day / I opened the newspaper,

／そして ／そこにあった 私の 先生の 笑っている 顔。
/ and / there was my teacher's smiling face.

⑥それ だった 私の 絵
It was my picture!

⑦私 だった とても 誇り ／の それ。
I was very proud / of it,

／そして そう だった 私の 先生。
/ and so was my teacher.

❖ 覚えよう

B1 **Could you describe the best picture you've ever drawn?**

I once drew a picture of my teacher when I was in elementary school. My picture showed him teaching our class with a big smile on his face. I sent the picture to a newspaper for children that I used to read. They sometimes posted pictures. To my surprise, one day I opened the newspaper, and there was my teacher's smiling face. It was my picture! I was very proud of it, and so was my teacher.

❖ 話してみよう

A1 Do you like to paint?

A2 Who is your favorite artist, and why do you like this person?

B1 In your opinion, why is Vincent Van Gogh so famous?

43 Crafts
工芸

❖ 質問しよう

A1 今まで陶芸をしたことがありますか。
Have you ever made pottery?

A2 日本で陶芸が有名な場所を教えてください。
What are some areas in Japan that are famous for pottery?

B1 日本の陶芸が他の種類の陶芸と異なる点は何ですか。
What distinguishes Japanese pottery from other kinds of pottery?

❖ 答えよう

A1 Have you ever made pottery?
はい。// いいえ。// はい、あります。// いいえ、ありません。// 一度。// 一度も。
Yes. // No. // Yes, I have. // No, I haven't. // One time. // Never.

A2 What are some areas in Japan that are famous for pottery?
私は陶芸で有名な場所は、京都と滋賀の2つの場所しか知りません。
I know only two places that are famous for pottery: Kyoto and Shiga.

B1 What distinguishes Japanese pottery from other kinds of pottery?
①私は日本の陶芸が他の種類の陶芸と異なる大きな点は、質素さが強調されていることです。
I think the major point by which Japanese pottery can be distinguished from other kinds of pottery is its emphasis on simplicity.

②日本の陶芸は概して明るい色を使わず、あるいは釣り合いさえとれていません。
Japanese pottery isn't typically bright or even symmetrical.

③より暗く、微妙な色遣い、そして均整の取れていない形が好まれます。
Darker, subtler colors and uneven shapes are preferred.

④もちろん、これは陶芸の種類にもよりますが、私は、多かれ少なかれ日本の陶芸の典型的な特徴だと思います。
Of course, this differs from one type of pottery to another, but I believe these are, more or less, the typical features of Japanese pottery.

❖ 練習しよう：❶ 単語ごとに英訳しよう
　　　　　　　❷「/」ごとに英訳しよう

B1 What distinguishes Japanese pottery from other kinds of pottery?

①私　思う　/その　メジャーな　ポイント　/によって　その
I think / the major point / by which

/日本の　陶芸　できる　だ　区別される
/ Japanese pottery can be distinguished

/から　他の　種類　の　陶芸　/だ　それの　強調　に　単純さ。
/ from other kinds of pottery / is its emphasis on simplicity.

②日本の　陶芸　でない　典型的に　明るい　/または　さえ　対称的。
Japanese pottery isn't typically bright / or even symmetrical.

③より暗い　より微妙な　色　/そして　凸凹のある　形　/だ　好まれる。
Darker, subtler colors / and uneven shapes / are preferred.

④もちろん　/これ　異なる　/から　1つの　タイプ　の　陶芸
Of course, / this differs / from one type of pottery

/に　もう1つ　/しかし　/私　信じる　これら　だ　/多かれ少なかれ
/ to another, / but / I believe these are, / more or less,

/その　典型的な　特徴　の　日本の　陶芸。
/ the typical features of Japanese pottery.

43 Crafts 工芸

❖ 覚えよう

B1 **What distinguishes Japanese pottery from other kinds of pottery?**

I think the major point by which Japanese pottery can be distinguished from other kinds of pottery is its emphasis on simplicity. Japanese pottery isn't typically bright or even symmetrical. Darker, subtler colors and uneven shapes are preferred. Of course, this differs from one type of pottery to another, but I believe these are, more or less, the typical features of Japanese pottery.

❖ 話してみよう

A1 Do you like to make things with your hands?
A2 What kinds of crafts are common in Japan?
B1 What kind of Japanese craft would you give as a gift to someone from another country and why?

44 Photography
写真

❖ 質問しよう

> A1 あなたは写真を撮ることが好きですか。
> Do you like taking pictures?
>
> A2 あなたは何の写真を撮ることが好きですか。
> What do you like to take pictures of?
>
> B1 なぜ多くの日本人が写真を撮るときピースサインをすると思いますか。
> Why do so many Japanese people show the peace sign when having their picture taken?

❖ 答えよう

A1 Do you like taking pictures?
はい。// いいえ。// はい、好きです。// いいえ、好きではありません。// もちろん。// あまり。
Yes. // No. // Yes, I do. // No, I don't. // Of course. // Not really.

A2 What do you like to take pictures of?
私は友達の写真を撮ることが好きです。
I like to take pictures of my friends.

B1 Why do so many Japanese people show the peace sign when having their picture taken?

①以前に同じことを聞かれたことがあります。
I have been asked that before.

②最初、私は知らなかったのですが、調べてみてわかりました。それは60年代のヒッピー文化の間に西洋からきたものです。
At first I didn't know, but I researched it and found out that it came from western countries during the hippie culture of the 60's.

③それは元々は平和を意味しましたが、我々日本人は、それをカメラの前で自身を表現するための1つの方法として使い始めました。
Although it originally meant "peace," we Japanese started using it as a way to express ourselves in front of the camera.

④そして、ピースサインを作ることで、写真を撮る人に準備ができたことを知らせるのです。
And making the peace sign lets the photographer know that everyone is ready.

❖ 練習しよう：❶ 単語ごとに英訳しよう
　　　　　　❷「/」ごとに英訳しよう

B1 Why do so many Japanese people show the peace sign when having their picture taken?

①私　持つ　だった　尋ねた　それ　/ 以前に。
I have been asked that / before.

②最初は　/ 私　なかった　知る　/ しかし　/ 私　調べた　それ
At first / I didn't know, / but / I researched it

/ そして　見つけ出した
/ and found out

/ ということ　それ　来た　から　西洋の　国
/ that it came from western countries

/ 間　その　ヒッピー　文化　/ の　その　60年代。
/ during the hippie culture / of the 60's.

③けれども　それ　元々は　意味した　平和
Although it originally meant "peace,"

/ 我々　日本人　スタートした　/ 使うこと　それ
we Japanese started / using it

/ として　1つの　方法　/ 表現すること　我々自身
/ as a way / to express ourselves

/ の前で　その　カメラ。
/ in front of the camera.

④そして / 作ること その ピースサイン
And / making the peace sign

/ させる その 撮影者 知る / ということ みな だ 準備できる。
/ lets the photographer know / that everyone is ready.

❖ 覚えよう

B1 **Why do so many Japanese people show the peace sign when having their picture taken?**

I have been asked that before. At first I didn't know, but I researched it and found out that it came from western countries during the hippie culture of the 60's. Although it originally meant "peace," we Japanese started using it as a way to express ourselves in front of the camera. And making the peace sign lets the photographer know that everyone is ready.

❖ 話してみよう

A1 Do you ever post pictures on social media site, like Facebook?

A2 What kinds of photographs do you like to look at?

B1 How has the world changed now that so many people have cell phones with cameras with them at all times?

45 Movies & Theater
映画・演劇

❖ 質問しよう

> **A1** あなたの大好きな映画俳優は誰ですか。
> Who is your favorite movie star?
>
> **A2** あなたはどんな映画が好きですか。
> What kind of movies do you like?
>
> **B1** あなたが最近観た映画の内容を教えてください。
> Would you describe the last movie you watched?

❖ 答えよう

A1 Who is your favorite movie star?

ジョニー・デップ。

Johnny Depp.

A2 What kind of movies do you like?

私は面白い内容で面白い登場人物が登場するおかしい映画が好きです。

I like funny movies that have good stories and interesting characters.

B1 Would you describe the last movie you watched?

①最後に観た映画ですか？

The last movie I watched?

②最近たくさん映画を観ていますが、観た映画のタイトルを思い出せません。

I've seen a lot of movies lately, but I can't remember the title of the most recent one.

③それは、実際、コメディーで、友人グループの1人が結婚するので、みなで楽しい時を過ごそうとする映画でした。

It was actually a comedy about a group of friends who want to have a good time because one of them is getting married.

④たくさんクレイジーなことが一緒にいる間に起きました。
　Many crazy things happened during their time together.
⑤それは本当に面白い映画で、たくさん笑ってしまいました。
　It was really a good movie and made me laugh a lot.
⑥あなたにもお勧めです。
　You should see it.
⑦そのタイトルさえ思い出せればよいのですが。
　Now, if I could only remember the name...

❖ 練習しよう：❶ 単語ごとに英訳しよう
　　　　　　　❷「 / 」ごとに英訳しよう

B1 **Would you describe the last movie you watched?**

①その　最後の　映画　/ 私　観た。
　The last movie / I watched?

②私持つ　見た　たくさんの　映画　/ 最近
　I've seen a lot of movies / lately,

　/ しかし　/ 私は　できない　思い出す
　/ but / I can't remember

　/ その　タイトル　の　その　最も　最近の　1つ。
　/ the title of the most recent one.

③それ　だった　実際に　1つの　コメディー
　It was actually a comedy

　/ について　1つの　グループ　の　友達
　/ about a group of friends

　/ その人たち　ほしい　持つこと　1つの　よい　時間
　/ who want to have a good time

　/ なぜなら　1つ　の　彼ら　/ だ　なっている　結婚する。
　/ because one of them / is getting married.

④多くの　クレイジーな　こと　起こった　/ 間に　彼らの　時間　一緒に。
　Many crazy things happened / during their time together.

⑤それ だった 本当に 1つの よい 映画
It was really a good movie

/そして させた 私を 笑う たくさん。
/ and made me laugh a lot.

⑥あなた べき 見る それ。
You should see it.

⑦今 /もし 私 できた 唯一 思い出す /その 名前。
Now, / if I could only remember / the name...

❖ 覚えよう

B1 **Would you describe the last movie you watched?**

The last movie I watched? I've seen a lot of movies lately, but I can't remember the title of the most recent one. It was actually a comedy about a group of friends who want to have a good time because one of them is getting married. Many crazy things happened during their time together. It was really a good movie and made me laugh a lot. You should see it. Now, if I could only remember the name...

❖ 話してみよう

A1 Have you ever seen a play?
A2 What kinds of plays are you interested in?
B1 Could you describe a play that you know about?

46 Skills Acquisition
芸道

❖ 質問しよう

> **A1** 今までに書道を習ったことがありますか。
> Have you ever learned calligraphy?
>
> **A2** 日本の書道をするのに必要な道具は何ですか。
> What items do you need in order to do Japanese calligraphy?
>
> **B1** 日本の書道を外国人に説明してください。
> How would you describe Japanese calligraphy to a foreigner?

❖ 答えよう

A1 Have you ever learned calligraphy?
はい。// いいえ。// はい、あります。// いいえ、ありません。// 小学校で。

Yes. // No. // Yes, I have. // No, I haven't. // In elementary school.

A2 What items do you need in order to do Japanese calligraphy?
筆はもちろん、すずり、半紙、文珍、下敷き、そして印など、いくつかのものが必要です。

You need several things: a brush, of course, an inkstone, special paper, a paperweight, a cloth and a seal.

B1 How would you describe Japanese calligraphy to a foreigner?
①書道は元々中国から伝わりましたが、現在では、ひらがなやカタカナが漢字に混じっています。

It originally came from China, but now *hiragana* and *katakana* are mixed with *kanji*.

②日本の書道は1つの芸術の形で、それは仏教から大きな影響を受けました。
Japanese calligraphy is an art form, and it was influenced by Buddhism very much.

③書道をする人は、書くチャンスは一度きりです。というのは、訂正することが許されないからです。
The person doing the calligraphy has only one chance to write the characters because correction is not allowed.

④ある意味、どのように書を書くかは、その当時の書き手の思考を表します。だから書を書く過程はとても霊的なものだと言えます。
In a way, how one does the calligraphy represents the thinking of the writer at that time, so you can say that the process of doing it is very spiritual.

❖ 練習しよう：❶ 単語ごとに英訳しよう
　　　　　　　❷「/」ごとに英訳しよう

B1 How would you describe Japanese calligraphy to a foreigner?

①それ　元々　来た　から　中国　/しかし　今
It originally came from China, / but now

/ひらがな　そして　カタカナ　だ　混ぜられる
/ *hiragana* and *katakana* are mixed

/と一緒に　漢字。
/ with *kanji*.

②日本の　書道　だ　/1つの　芸術　形　/そして
Japanese calligraphy is / an art form, / and

/それ　だった　影響される　/によって　仏教　/とても　多く。
/ it was influenced / by Buddhism / very much.

③その　人　している　その　書道/持つ　唯一　1つの　チャンス
The person doing the calligraphy / has only one chance

/ため　書く　その　文字　/なぜなら　訂正　だ　ない　許される。
/ to write the characters / because correction is not allowed.

④ある意味 / どのように 1人 する その 書道
In a way, / how one does the calligraphy

/ 表す その 考えること / の その 書き手 / で その 時
/ represents the thinking / of the writer / at that time,

/ だから あなた できる 言う
/ so you can say

/ ということ その プロセス の すること それ
/ that the process of doing it

/ だ とても 霊的。
/ is very spiritual.

❖ 覚えよう

B1 **How would you describe Japanese calligraphy to a foreigner?**

It originally came from China, but now *hiragana* and *katakana* are mixed with *kanji*. Japanese calligraphy is an art form, and it was influenced by Buddhism very much. The person doing the calligraphy has only one chance to write the characters because correction is not allowed. In a way, how one does the calligraphy represents the thinking of the writer at that time, so you can say that the process of doing it is very spiritual.

❖ 話してみよう

A1 Do you like learning new skills?

A2 What is one new skill you'd like to learn?

B1 How would you teach a basic skill, like using chopsticks, to a child?

47 Art in General
芸術一般

❖ 質問しよう

> **A1** あなたの好きな画家は誰ですか。
> Who is your favorite painter?
>
> **A2** あなたのお気に入りの絵について話してください。
> Can you talk about your favorite painting?
>
> **B1** 芸術とは何か説明してください。
> Could you explain what art is?

❖ 答えよう

A1 **Who is your favorite painter?**
ピカソです。// モネです // ゴッホです。
Picasso. // Monet. // Van Gogh.

A2 **Can you talk about your favorite painting?**
私のお気に入りの絵は、ゴッホの「星月夜」です。
My favorite painting is *The Starry Night* by Vincent Van Gogh.

B1 **Could you explain what art is?**

① 一般的な用語としての芸術には、人間が創造するほとんどのものが含まれる可能性があります。

Art, as a general term, can include almost anything created by a human being.

② しかし、美術は手で触れられる作品しか含みません。

Fine art, however, includes only works we can touch.

③ 絵画、彫刻、建築は美術に含まれますが、音楽、文学、映画は含まれません。

Painting, sculpture, and architecture are included in fine art whereas music, literature and movies are not.

④書道は美術に含まれますが、小説は含まれません。
   Calligraphy is included in fine art whereas novels are not.
⑤書道においては、文字の見た目が重要です。
   In calligraphy, the visual appearance of the characters is important.
⑥それとは対照的に、小説にとっては、文字で表現された内容が文字そのものよりはるかに重要です。
   In contrast, for a novel, the content expressed by the letters is much more important than the letters themselves.

❖ 練習しよう：❶ 単語ごとに英訳しよう
　　　　　　　❷「／」ごとに英訳しよう

B1 Could you explain what art is?

①芸術　／として　1つの　一般的な　用語　／できる　含む
   Art, / as a general term, / can include

／ほとんど　何でも　／創造される　によって　1つの　人間。
   / almost anything / created by a human being.

②美術　／しかしながら　／含む　だけ　作品　／私たち　できる　触る。
   Fine art, / however, / includes only works / we can touch.

③絵画　／彫刻　／そして　建築　／だ　含まれる　／に　美術
   Painting, / sculpture, / and architecture / are included / in fine art

／一方　／音楽　／文学　／そして　映画　／だ　ない。
   / whereas / music, / literature / and movies / are not.

④書道　だ　含まれる　／に　美術　／一方　／小説　だ　ない。
   Calligraphy is included / in fine art / whereas / novels are not.

⑤に　書道　／その　視覚上の　外見　／の　その　文字
   In calligraphy, / the visual appearance / of the characters

／だ　重要。
   / is important.

⑥対照的に　／にとって　1つの　小説　／その　内容
   In contrast, / for a novel, / the content

/ 表現される　によって　その　文字 / だ　ずっと　より　重要
/ expressed by the letters / is much more important

/ よりも　その　文字　それら自身。
/ than the letters themselves.

❖ 覚えよう

B1 **Could you explain what art is?**

Art, as a general term, can include almost anything created by a human being. Fine art, however, includes only works we can touch. Painting, sculpture, and architecture are included in fine art whereas music, literature and movies are not. Calligraphy is included in fine art whereas novels are not. In calligraphy, the visual appearance of the characters is important. In contrast, for a novel, the content expressed by the letters is much more important than the letters themselves.

❖ 話してみよう

> **A1** Do you like art?
> **A2** What is your favorite form of art?
> **B1** In your opinion, why do humans create art?

48 Hobbies
趣味

❖ **質問しよう**

> **A1** あなたは暇な時何をすることが好きですか。
> What do you like to do in your free time?
>
> **A2** もっと自由な時間があったら、あなたは何をしたいですか。
> What would you like to do if you had more free time?
>
> **B1** 友達が暇で何か新しい趣味がほしいと言ったら、あなたはどんなことを提案しますか。
> If a friend told you she was bored and wanted a new hobby, what would you suggest?

❖ **答えよう**

A1 **What do you like to do in your free time?**
漫画を読むことです。
Reading manga.

A2 **What would you like to do if you had more free time?**
もしもっと自由な時間があったら、たぶんその時間を美味しい食事を作ることに当てると思います。でも、そうするための時間がありません。
If I had more free time, I'd probably spend it cooking nice meals. I just don't have the time to do it now.

B1 **If a friend told you she was bored and wanted a new hobby, what would you suggest?**
①もし友達が私につまらないと言ったら、私は彼女に近所の何らかの教室やワークショップを探すことを勧めます。
If a friend told me she was bored, I'd suggest that she look for some kind of class or workshop in her area.

②いくつか例を挙げると、絵画、写真それから陶芸のようなたくさんの異なる種類の教室があります。

There are classes for many different kinds of things like painting, photography and pottery to name a few.

③もし彼女がこのような教室に参加することによって、ひょっとするとまったく新しい趣味を見つけたり、面白い人々に出会ったりすることがあるかもしれません。

If she participates in something like this, she might find a great new hobby, and she might meet some interesting people, too.

❖ 練習しよう：❶ 単語ごとに英訳しよう
　　　　　　❷「／」ごとに英訳しよう

B1 If a friend told you she was bored and wanted a new hobby, what would you suggest?

①もし　1人の　友達　言った　私／彼女　だった　退屈

If a friend told me / she was bored,

／私だろう　提案する　／それ　彼女　探す　／ある　種類　の　クラス
／ I'd suggest / that she look for / some kind of class

／または　ワークショップ　／中に　彼女の　エリア。
／ or workshop / in her area.

②そこに　ある　クラス　／ための　多くの　異なった　種類　の　こと

There are classes / for many different kinds of things

／ような　絵画　写真　そして　陶芸
／ like painting, photography and pottery

ために　名前を挙げる　2、3。
／ to name a few.

③もし　彼女が　参加する　／中に　何か　ような　これ

If she participates / in something like this,

／彼女　かもしれなかった　見つける　／1つの　偉大な　新しい　趣味
／ she might find / a great new hobby,

/ そして / 彼女は かもしれなかった 会う
/ and / she might meet

/ いくつかの 面白い 人々 も。
/ some interesting people, too.

❖ 覚えよう

B1 **If a friend told you she was bored and wanted a new hobby, what would you suggest?**

If a friend told me she was bored, I'd suggest that she look for some kind of class or workshop in her area. There are classes for many different kinds of things like painting, photography and pottery to name a few. If she participates in something like this, she might find a great new hobby, and she might meet some interesting people, too.

❖ 話してみよう

> **A1** What is your hobby?
> **A2** When did you begin your hobby?
> **B1** Could you tell me about your hobby in detail?

49 Collections
コレクション

❖ 質問しよう

> **A1** あなたはぬいぐるみを集めたことがありますか。
> Have you ever collected stuffed toys?
>
> **A2** 子供のころ、あなたはどんなコレクションをしていましたか。
> What kind of collection did you have when you were a child?
>
> **B1** 面白いコレクションをしている人について、話してください。
> Would you tell me about someone who has an interesting collection?

❖ 答えよう

A1 **Have you ever collected stuffed toys?**
はい。// いいえ。// はい、あります。// いいえ、ありません。// 集めていました。
Yes. // No. // Yes, I have. // No, I haven't. // I used to.

A2 **What kind of collection did you have when you were a child?**
ぬいぐるみを集めていました。
I used to collect stuffed toys.

B1 **Would you tell me about someone who has an interesting collection?**
①私にはフクロウを集めている友達がいます。
I have a friend who collects owls.

②彼女は、フクロウのように見える物やフクロウの模様なら何でも集めます。
She collects anything that looks like an owl or has an owl pattern.

③彼女はフクロウのシャツやセーターまで持っています。
　She even has shirts and sweaters with owls on them.
④それに、カップ、皿、タオルも持っています。
　She has cups, plates, and towels, too.
⑤彼女は、終わらない宝探しをしているようだと私は思います。
　I think it's like a never-ending treasure hunt for her.
⑥だから、彼女がそれをしていると私は思うのです。
　That's why I think she does it.
⑦彼女はいつも次のフクロウを探しているので、彼女にとっては、人生はいつも冒険です。
　For her, life is always an adventure because she's always looking for the next owl.

❖ 練習しよう：❶ 単語ごとに英訳しよう
　　　　　　❷「／」ごとに英訳しよう

B1 Would you tell me about someone who has an interesting collection?

①私は　持つ　1つの　友達　／その人　集める　フクロウ。
　I have a friend / who collects owls.
②彼女　集める　何でも　／それ　見える　ように　1つの　フクロウ
　She collects anything / that looks like an owl

　／または　持つ　1つの　フクロウ　模様。
　／ or has an owl pattern.
③彼女　さえ　持つ　シャツ　／そして　セーター
　She even has shirts / and sweaters

　／と一緒に　フクロウ　に　それら。
　／ with owls on them.
④彼女は　持つ　カップ　／皿　／そして　タオル　も。
　She has cups, / plates, / and towels, too.
⑤私　思う　／それだ　のよう　1つの　終わらない　宝探し
　I think / it's like a never-ending treasure hunt

/にとって 彼女。
/ for her.

⑥それだ なぜ /私 思う 彼女 する それ。
That's why / I think she does it.

⑦にとって 彼女に /人生 だ いつも 1つの アドベンチャー
For her, / life is always an adventure

/なぜなら 彼女だ いつも /探している その 次の フクロウ。
/ because she's always / looking for the next owl.

❖ 覚えよう

B1 **Would you tell me about someone who has an interesting collection?**

I have a friend who collects owls. She collects anything that looks like an owl or has an owl pattern. She even has shirts and sweaters with owls on them. She has cups, plates, and towels, too. I think it's like a never-ending treasure hunt for her. That's why I think she does it. For her, life is always an adventure because she's always looking for the next owl.

❖ 話してみよう

> **A1** Do you have any kind of collection?
> **A2** What are some common things that people collect?
> **B1** If you started a new collection, what would you choose to collect and why?

50 DIY
日曜大工

❖ 質問しよう

A1 今までに家具を作ったことがありますか。
Have you ever made a piece of furniture?

A2 今までにしたことのある DIY のプロジェクトを教えてください。
Could you describe a DIY project you have done?

B1 あなたはなぜ今日 DIY がとても人気があると思いますか。
Why do you think DIY projects are so popular these days?

❖ 答えよう

A1 Have you ever made a piece of furniture?
はい。// いいえ。// はい、あります。// いいえ、ありません。// 一度も。
Yes. // No. // Yes, I have. // No, I haven't. // No, never.

A2 Could you describe a DIY project you have done?
私はかつてリサイクル品から木製の椅子を作ったことがあります。
I once made a wooden chair from recycled materials.

B1 Why do you think DIY projects are so popular these days?
①えー、昔よりも今の方が人々に時間的ゆとりがあり、そして、インターネットや店で開かれている DIY 教室で、ものづくりの方法をより簡単に学ぶことができるようになったと思います。

Well, I think people have more time now than in the past, and it's easier now to learn how to make things on the internet or in the DIY classes offered at some stores.

②また、多くの人々がお店で買えるものよりも手作りの製品を評価して大事にします。

Also, many people seem to appreciate and cherish handmade products over things that can be bought at a store.

③それはお金を節約するというよりもむしろ、個性的でユニークなものを作ることに関連していると思います。

It's not so much an issue of saving money but has more to do with creating something personal and unique.

④以上のことが、それを特別なものにしているのです。

That's what makes it special.

❖ 練習しよう：❶ 単語ごとに英訳しよう
　　　　　　❷「 / 」ごとに英訳しよう

B1 Why do you think DIY projects are so popular these days?

①えー /私 思う /人々 持つ より多い 時間 今
Well, / I think / people have more time now

/よりも に その 過去 /そして それだ より簡単 今
/ than in the past, / and it's easier now

/学ぶこと /いかに 作ること 物 /の上で その インターネット
/ to learn / how to make things / on the internet

/または に その DIY 教室 /提供される に いくつかの 店。
/ or in the DIY classes / offered at some stores.

②また /多くの 人々 ようだ 評価すること /そして 大事にする
Also, / many people seem to appreciate / and cherish

/手作りの 製品 /超えて 物 /それ できる だ 買われる
/ handmade products / over things / that can be bought

/で 1つの 店。
/ at a store.

③それだ ない そんなに 多く 1つの 問題 /の 節約する お金
It's not so much an issue / of saving money

/しかし 持つ より多く ため する と一緒に
/ but has more to do with

/創造すること 何か 個人的な /そして 独特な。
/ creating something personal / and unique.

④ それだ / 何 作る それ 特別。
　That's / what makes it special.

❖ 覚えよう

B1 **Why do you think DIY projects are so popular these days?**

Well, I think people have more time now than in the past, and it's easier now to learn how to make things on the internet or in the DIY classes offered at some stores. Also, many people seem to appreciate and cherish handmade products over things that can be bought at a store. It's not so much an issue of saving money but has more to do with creating something personal and unique. That's what makes it special.

❖ 話してみよう

A1 Which would you prefer, ready-made furniture or furniture that has been made by a friend or relative?

A2 What is a reason someone might prefer handmade furniture to ready-made furniture?

B1 Could you describe the difference between handmade furniture and ready-made furniture?

51 Handicraft
手芸

❖ 質問しよう

> **A1** 今までに宝飾品を作ったことがありますか。
> Have you ever made jewelry?
>
> **A2** あなたが今までにあげた、あるいはもらったことのある手作りのプレゼントを教えてください。
> Could you describe a handmade gift you have given or received?
>
> **B1** あなたは手作りのプレゼントと既製品のプレゼントどちらを好みますか。それはなぜですか。
> Which do you prefer and why: handmade gifts or store-bought gifts?

❖ 答えよう

A1 **Have you ever made jewelry?**
はい。// いいえ。// いいえ、ありません。// はい、ネックレスです。
Yes. // No. // Yes, I have. // Yes, a necklace.

A2 **Could you describe a handmade gift you have given or received?**
1度私は妹のために絵を書きました。彼女はそれが本当に好きでした。
Once I painted a picture for my sister. She really loved it.

B1 **Which do you prefer and why: handmade gifts or store-bought gifts?**
①私は普段とても忙しくて手作りの品を作ることはできないのですが、手作りの贈り物をもらうことは好きです。
Though I am usually too busy to make them, I love receiving handmade gifts.

②手作りの品をもらった時には、その中にたくさんの思いが詰まっていることがわかります。

When I get one, I realize a lot of consideration went into the making of it.

③もしその人が私にとって特別な人なら、私は贈り物を作るよう精一杯努力します。

If the person is special to me, then I will try hard to make a gift.

④それは、すべて時間があるか否かにかかってきます。

It all comes down to time.

⑤残念ながら、何か特別な物を作る時間がとれないことがしばしばです。

Unfortunately, I don't often have enough time to make something special.

❖ 練習しよう：❶ 単語ごとに英訳しよう　　❷「/」ごとに英訳しよう

B1 Which do you prefer and why: handmade gifts or store-bought gifts?

①とはいえ /私 だ いつも あまりに 忙しい /作ること それら
Though / I am usually too busy / to make them,

/私 愛する 受け取ること /手作りの ギフト。
/ I love receiving / handmade gifts.

②時 私 得る 1つ /私 わかる /たくさんの 考慮
When I get one, / I realize / a lot of consideration

/行った の中に その 作ること の それ。
/ went into the making of it.

③もし その 人 /だ 特別な に 私 /それから
If the person / is special to me, / then

/私 だろう トライする ハードに /作ること 1つの ギフト。
/ I will try hard / to make a gift.

④それ すべて 来る 下に /に 時間。
It all comes down / to time.

153

⑤不運にも / 私　ない　しばしば / 持つ　十分な　時間
Unfortunately, / I don't often / have enough time
/ ため　作る　何か　特別な。
/ to make something special.

❖ 覚えよう

B1 **Which do you prefer and why: handmade gifts or store-bought gifts?**

Though I am usually too busy to make them, I love receiving handmade gifts. When I get one, I realize a lot of consideration went into the making of it. If the person is special to me, then I will try hard to make a gift. It all comes down to time. Unfortunately, I don't often have enough time to make something special.

❖ 話してみよう

A1 Can you make *origami*?

A2 What's the most interesting piece of origami you've ever seen?

B1 Could you explain the significance of origami cranes?

52 Gambling
ギャンブル

❖ 質問しよう

A1 あなたは今までに友達とかけをしたことがありますか。
Have you ever made a bet with a friend?

A2 人気のあるギャンブルは何ですか。
What are some popular kinds of gambling?

B1 どうしてギャンブルは人気があるのか、意見を聞かせてください。
In your opinion, why is gambling so popular?

❖ 答えよう

A1 **Have you ever made a bet with a friend?**
はい。// いいえ。// はい、あります。// いいえ、ありません。// もちろん。
Yes. // No. // Yes, I have. // No, I haven't. // Sure.

A2 **What are some popular kinds of gambling?**
人気のあるギャンブルは、競馬、ポーカーそしてパチンコです。
Some popular kinds of gambling are horse races, poker and *pachinko*.

B1 **In your opinion, why is gambling so popular?**
①ギャンブルは麻薬のように中毒になると言います。
They say that gambling is addictive like a drug.

②スリルを味わえるので、1度始めるとやめるのはとても難しいです。
Once you get started, it's difficult to stop because of the thrill it gives you.

③毎回の決断が一瞬の満足になります。
Every decision can result in instant gratification.

④お金持ちになることも可能です。
You could become rich.

⑤もちろん、その決断ですべてを失うことにもなるのですが、それも魅力の1つです。
Of course, you can lose with every decision, too, but that's part of the allure.

⑥ギャンブルが好きな人は、たくさんのお金を得る可能性にしばしば心をひかれます。とはいえ、それをすべて失うこともあるのですが。
Those people who like to gamble are often attracted to the possibility of winning a lot of money, though they may lose it all.

❖ 練習しよう：❶ 単語ごとに英訳しよう
　　　　　　❷「／」ごとに英訳しよう

B1 In your opinion, why is gambling so popular?

①彼ら　言う　／ということ　ギャンブル　だ　中毒的
They say / that gambling is addictive

／ように　1つの　薬。
/ like a drug.

②1度　あなた　得る　スタートした
Once you get started,

／それだ　難しい　ストップすること
/ it's difficult to stop

／のせいで　その　スリル　／それ　与える　あなた。
/ because of the thrill / it gives you.

③すべての　決定　できる　結果する　／に　瞬間の　満足。
Every decision can result / in instant gratification.

④あなた　できた　なる　金持ち。
You could become rich.

⑤もちろん　／あなた　できる　失う　／と一緒に　すべての　決定　／も
Of course, / you can lose / with every decision, / too,

／しかし　／それだ　部分　の　その　魅惑。
/ but / that's part of the allure.

⑥それらの 人々 /その人々 好きだ ギャンブルすること
Those people / who like to gamble

/だ よく 魅了される /に その 可能性
/ are often attracted / to the possibility

/の 勝つこと たくさんの お金
/ of winning a lot of money,

/とはいえ 彼ら かもしれない 失う それ すべて。
/ though they may lose it all.

❖ 覚えよう

B1 **In your opinion, why is gambling so popular?**

They say that gambling is addictive like a drug. Once you get started, it's difficult to stop because of the thrill it gives you. Every decision can result in instant gratification. You could become rich. Of course, you can lose with every decision, too, but that's part of the allure. Those people who like to gamble are often attracted to the possibility of winning a lot of money, though they may lose it all.

❖ 話してみよう

A1 Have you ever watched a horse race?
A2 What kinds of people like to gamble?
B1 What would happen if all forms of gambling were made illegal?

53 Games
遊び・ゲーム

❖ **質問しよう**

> A1 あなたは子供のころどんなゲームをよくしましたか。
> What game did you like to play in your childhood?
>
> A2 ほとんどの子供たちはどんなゲームが好きですか。
> What kind of game do most children like?
>
> B1 あなたが子供のころ一番好きだったゲームや活動を教えてください。
> Could you describe the game or activity you liked best in your childhood?

❖ **答えよう**

A1 **What game did you like to play in your childhood?**
人生ゲームです。//「人生ゲーム」と呼ばれるゲームです。
Life. // A game called "Life."

A2 **What kind of game do most children like?**
テレビゲームが好きです。
They like video games.

B1 **Could you describe the game or activity you liked best in your childhood?**

①えー、私は友達と外で遊ぶことは本当に好きでした。
Well, I really liked playing outside with my friends.

②よくやったのは「どろけい」でした。
What we played a lot was cops and robbers.

③私たちは2つのグループを作り、1つのグループが泥棒そして残りが警察になりました。
We would make two groups—one for robbers and the other for police.

④それから、泥棒のグループが隠れて、警察のグループが捕まえます。
　　Then the group of robbers would hide and the group of police would try to catch them.
　　⑤「どろけい」はチームワークが必要で、とても楽しかったです。
　　It required teamwork, and it was a lot of fun.

❖ 練習しよう：❶ 単語ごとに英訳しよう
　　　　　　❷「／」ごとに英訳しよう

B1 Could you describe the game or activity you liked best in your childhood?

①えー ／私 本当に 好きだった 遊ぶこと 外で
　Well, / I really liked playing outside
／と一緒に 私の 友達。
／with my friends.
②何 私たち 遊んだ たくさん ／だった どろけい。
　What we played a lot / was cops and robbers.
③私たち ～たものだ 作る ２つの グループ ／１つ のため 泥棒
　We would make two groups / —one for robbers
／そして もう１つ のため 警察。
／and the other for police.
④それから ／その グループ の 泥棒 ／～たものだ 隠れる ／そして
　Then / the group of robbers / would hide / and
／その グループ の 警察
／the group of police
／～たものだ トライする 捕まえる 彼ら。
／would try to catch them.
⑤それ 要求した チームワーク
　It required teamwork,
／そして それ だった たくさんの 楽しみ。
／and it was a lot of fun.

159

❖ 覚えよう

B1 **Could you describe the game or activity you liked best in your childhood?**

Well, I really liked playing outside with my friends. What we played a lot was cops and robbers. We would make two groups—one for robbers and the other for police. Then the group of robbers would hide and the group of police would try to catch them. It required teamwork, and it was a lot of fun.

❖ 話してみよう

> **A1** Do you play games on your phone?
>
> **A2** What are some popular games people play on their phones?
>
> **B1** What are some of the good and bad points of playing games on your phone?

54 Religion
宗教

❖ 質問しよう

A1 今までに神社に行ったことがありますか。
Have you ever been to a shrine?

A2 日本で最も一般的な宗教は何ですか。
What is the most common religion in Japan?

B1 神道と仏教はどう違いますか。
How are Shintoism and Buddhism different?

❖ 答えよう

A1 Have you ever been to a shrine?
はい。// いいえ。// はい、あります。// いいえ、ありません。// はい、明治神宮です。
Yes. // No. // Yes, I have. // No, I haven't. // Yes, Meiji shrine.

A2 What is the most common religion in Japan?
日本で最も一般的な宗教は仏教です。
I think Buddhism is the most common religion in Japan.

B1 How are Shintoism and Buddhism different?
①それは答えるのがとても難しい質問です。なぜなら、その2つの宗教の間には、すごく多くの違いがあるからです。

That's a very difficult question to answer because there are so many differences between the two religions.

②しかし、簡単に答えると、神道と仏教の、全般的な哲学的アプローチの中に、主な違いがあると言えます。

To give a simple answer though, I would say that the main difference lies in the overall philosophical approach of Shintoism and Buddhism.

③神道は、赤ちゃんを近所の神社に連れて行ったり、そこで子供たちの七五三のお祝いをしたりというような「生」に関わる幸せな機会を連想させます。

Shintoism is associated with happy occasions related to the living, such as taking a new baby to the local Shinto shrine or celebrating the *shichi-go-san* ceremony for children there.

④一方、仏教は、葬式や悲しみの儀式を扱うような「死」にまつわる事柄と関係しています。

Buddhism, on the other hand, is concerned with matters of the dead, such as dealing with funerals or mourning ceremonies.

❖ 練習しよう：❶ 単語ごとに英訳しよう　　　　　　　　❷「／」ごとに英訳しよう

B1 How are Shintoism and Buddhism different?

①それだ　1つの　とても　難しい　質問　／ために　答える　／なぜなら
That's a very difficult question / to answer / because

／そこ　ある　そんなに　多い　違い　／間の　その　2つの　宗教。
/ there are so many differences / between the two religions.

②ために　与える　1つの　簡単な　答え　／とはいえ　／私　だろう　言う
To give a simple answer / though, / I would say

／ということ　その　主な　違い　横たわる
/ that the main difference lies

／に　その　全般的な　哲学的な　アプローチ　／の　神道　と　仏教。
/ in the overall philosophical approach / of Shintoism and Buddhism.

③神道　だ　連想される　と一緒に　幸せな　機会
Shintoism is associated with happy occasions

／関係する　に　その生　／　そんな　ような
/ related to the living, / such as

／連れていくこと　1つの　新しい　赤ちゃん　／に　その　近所の　神社
/ taking a new baby / to the local Shinto shrine

/または 祝っている その 七五三 儀式
/ or celebrating the *shichi-go-san* ceremony

/のため 子供たち そこで。
/ for children there.

④仏教 /その一方で /だ 関係している と一緒に 事柄
Buddhism, / on the other hand, / is concerned with matters

/の その 死 /そんな ような /扱うこと と一緒に 葬式
/ of the dead, / such as / dealing with funerals

/または 悲しんでいる 儀式。
/ or mourning ceremonies.

❖ 覚えよう

B1 **How are Shintoism and Buddhism different?**

That's a very difficult question to answer because there are so many differences between the two religions. To give a simple answer though, I would say that the main difference lies in the overall philosophical approach of Shintoism and Buddhism. Shintoism is associated with happy occasions related to the living, such as taking a new baby to the local Shinto shrine or celebrating the *shichi-go-san* ceremony for children there. Buddhism, on the other hand, is concerned with matters of the dead, such as dealing with funerals or mourning ceremonies.

❖ 話してみよう

A1 How do you say the word "religion" in your language?
A2 What is one difference between Buddhism and Christianity?
B1 What are some of the benefits of religion?

55 Festivals
祭り

❖ 質問しよう

> **A1** あなたは今までに夏祭りに行ったことがありますか。
> Have you ever been to a summer festival?
>
> **A2** 日本のお祭りで売っている一般的な食べ物は何ですか。
> What are some common foods sold at festivals in Japan?
>
> **B1** 今まで行ったお祭りの中で最も興味があるお祭りを説明してください。
> Could you describe one of the most interesting festivals you've been to?

❖ 答えよう

A1 **Have you ever been to a summer festival?**
はい。// いいえ。// はい、あります。// いいえ、ありません。// 一度も。
Yes. // No. // Yes, I have. // No, I haven't. // Never.

A2 **What are some common foods sold at festivals in Japan?**
お祭りの一般的な食べ物は、焼きそば、あるいはフライド・ヌードル、そして綿菓子、それはコットンキャンディです。
Common foods at festivals are things like *yakisoba*—or fried noodles—and *watagashi*, which is cotton candy.

B1 **Could you describe one of the most interesting festivals you've been to?**
①私は岸和田だんじり祭と呼ばれる祭りに行きました。それは毎年9月に大阪で行われます。
I went to a festival called Kishiwada Danjiri Matsuri, which is held every September in Osaka.

②この祭りの間、人々は山車を引っ張って狭い路地を歩きます。
For this festival, people pull floats through small streets.

③彼らは山車をとても速く、しかもとても狭い路地の中を引き歩くので、時々角を曲がり損ねて、家に突っ込んでしまうこともあります。

They pull the floats so fast down such narrow streets that they sometimes miss a corner and run into the houses.

④人が山車の上に乗り、いつ落ちるかわからないので、とてもスリルがあります。

It's especially thrilling because people ride on the top of the floats, and they could fall at any time.

❖ 練習しよう：❶ 単語ごとに英訳しよう
　　　　　　 ❷「 / 」ごとに英訳しよう

B1 Could you describe one of the most interesting festivals you've been to?

①私は 行った に 1つの 祭り /呼ばれる 岸和田だんじり祭

I went to a festival / called Kishiwada Danjiri Matsuri,

/それ だ 行われる すべての 9月 /に 大阪。

/ which is held every September / in Osaka.

②の間 この 祭り /人々 引く 山車

For this festival, / people pull floats

/を通って 小さな 通り。

/ through small streets.

③彼ら 引く その 山車 /そんなに 速く /下に

They pull the floats / so fast / down

/そんな 細い 通り /なので 彼ら 時々 ミスする 1つの 角

/ such narrow streets / that they sometimes miss a corner

/そして 走る の中を その 家。

/ and run into the houses.

④それだ 特別に スリリング /なぜなら 人々 乗る

It's especially thrilling / because people ride

/上に その トップ の その 山車

/ on the top of the floats,

/ そして　/ 彼ら　できた　落ちる　/ に　どんな　時。
/ and / they could fall /at any time.

❖ 覚えよう

B1 **Could you describe one of the most interesting festivals you've been to?**

I went to a festival called Kishiwada Danjiri Matsuri, which is held every September in Osaka. For this festival, people pull floats through small streets. They pull the floats so fast down such narrow streets that they sometimes miss a corner and run into the houses. It's especially thrilling because people ride on the top of the floats, and they could fall at any time.

❖ 話してみよう

A1 Do you like going to festivals?

A2 What are some of the most famous festivals in Japan?

B1 If you were asked to plan a unique school festival, what would you do?

56 History
歴史

❖ 質問しよう

> **A1** 明治時代の後の時代の名前は何ですか。
> What is the name of the period after the Meiji period?
>
> **A2** 明治時代は何年続きましたか。
> How many years did the Meiji period last?
>
> **B1** 江戸時代がどんな時代だったか教えてください。
> Could you describe the Edo period?

❖ 答えよう

A1 **What is the name of the period after the Meiji period?**
大正時代です。

The Taisho period.

A2 **How many years did the Meiji period last?**
それは 45 年続きました。

It lasted forty-five years.

B1 **Could you describe the Edo period?**
①江戸時代は日本史上最も長い時代の 1 つです。

The Edo period is one of the longest periods in Japanese history.

②それは徳川将軍の時代で、265 年続きました。

It was the age of the Tokugawa shogunate and lasted for two hundred and sixty-five years.

③江戸時代の特徴の 1 つは、鎖国、あるいはクローズド・ドア・ポリシーで、このため、日本はこの時代外国との接触がほとんどありませんでした。

One of the features of the Edo period is something called *sakoku*, or a closed-door policy, and because of this Japan had almost no contact with foreign countries during this time.

❖ 練習しよう：❶ 単語ごとに英訳しよう
　　　　　　　❷「 / 」ごとに英訳しよう

B1 Could you describe the Edo period?

①その　江戸時代　/ だ　1つ　その　最も長い　時代　/ に　日本の　歴史。
The Edo period / is one of the longest periods / in Japanese history.

②それ　だった　その　年　/ の　その　徳川将軍　/ そして　続いた
It was the age / of the Tokugawa shogunate / and lasted

/ の間　265年。
/ for two hundred and sixty-five years.

③1つ　の　その　特徴　の　江戸時代　/ だ　何か　呼ばれる　鎖国
One of the features of the Edo period / is something called *sakoku*,

/ または　1つの　クローズド・ドア・ポリシー
/ or a closed-door policy,

/ そして　のせいで　これ
/ and because of this

/ 日本　持った　ほとんど　ない　コンタクト
/ Japan had almost no contact

/ と一緒に　外国の　国　/ の間　この　時間。
/ with foreign countries / during this time.

❖ 覚えよう

B1 Could you describe the Edo period?

The Edo period is one of the longest periods in Japanese history. It was the age of the Tokugawa shogunate and lasted for two hundred and sixty-five years. One of the features of the Edo period is something called *sakoku*, or a closed-door policy, and because of this Japan had almost no contact with foreign countries during this time.

❖ 話してみよう

A1 Did you like studying history in high school?

A2 In your opinion, what is the most interesting period in Japanese history?

B1 Could you describe an important event in world history?

57 Media
メディア

❖ 質問しよう

> **A1** 週にどのくらいの時間テレビを見ますか。
> How many hours a week do you watch TV?
>
> **A2** あなたは普段いつテレビを見ますか。
> When do you usually watch TV?
>
> **B1** あなたが好きなテレビ番組について話してください。
> Would you describe a TV program that you like to watch?

❖ 答えよう

A1 **How many hours a week do you watch TV?**
3時間です。// 3、4時間だと思います。// 週にたった1時間です。
Three hours. // Three or four hours, I guess. // Only one hour a week.

A2 **When do you usually watch TV?**
私は普段夜に家族と一緒にテレビを見ます。
I usually watch TV in the evening with my family.

B1 **Would you describe a TV program that you like to watch?**
①私はテレビの旅番組を見ることが好きです。
I like to watch a TV program about traveling.

②ある有名人が、旅行先として有名でない小さな町を訪れて、面白いことを発見したり、山形の芋煮や福岡の明太子など、地方の美味しい食べ物を食べたりします。
Some celebrities visit small towns that are not popular traveling destinations and discover some interesting points or eat delicious regional foods, such as *imoni* in Yamagata or *mentaiko* in Fukuoka.

③そのような番組を見ると、旅や自分たちが住んでいる国について新しい発見ができます。

Those programs give us some new insights about traveling and the country we live in.

④またそれによって、これらの場所を訪れてみたくなります。

It makes me want to visit these places, too.

❖ 練習しよう：❶ 単語ごとに英訳しよう
　　　　　　❷「/」ごとに英訳しよう

B1 Would you describe a TV program that you like to watch?

①私　好きだ　見ること　１つの　テレビ番組

I like to watch a TV program

/について　旅行すること。

/ about traveling.

②何人かの　有名人　訪ねる　小さい　町

Some celebrities visit small towns

/それ　だ　ない　人気がある　旅行すること　目的地

/ that are not popular traveling destinations

/そして　発見する　いくつかの　興味深い　ポイント

/ and discover some interesting points

/または　食べる　美味しい　地方の　食べ物

/ or eat delicious regional foods,

/のような　芋煮　に　山形　/または　明太子　に　福岡。

/ such as *imoni* in Yamagata / or *mentaiko* in Fukuoka.

③それらの　プログラム　与える　私たち　/いくつかの　新しい　洞察

Those programs give us / some new insights

/について　旅行すること

/ about traveling

/そして　その　国　私たちが　住んでいる　に。

/ and the country we live in.

④それ させる 私 ほしい 訪ねること ／これらの 場所 も。
It makes me want to visit / these places, too.

❖ 覚えよう

B1 **Would you describe a TV program that you like to watch?**

I like to watch a TV program about traveling. Some celebrities visit small towns that are not popular traveling destinations and discover some interesting points or eat delicious regional foods, such as *imoni* in Yamagata or *mentaiko* in Fukuoka. Those programs give us some new insights about traveling and the country we live in. It makes me want to visit these places, too.

❖ 話してみよう

A1 Do you watch the news on TV?

A2 What is the most reliable news source?

B1 How has the internet changed the newspaper industry?

58 Show Business
芸能界

❖ 質問しよう

> **A1** 日本であなたの好きな有名人は誰ですか。
> Who is your favorite celebrity in Japan?
>
> **A2** あなたの好きな有名人の性格を説明してください。
> Could you describe the personality of your favorite Japanese celebrity?
>
> **B1** 日本で芸能人として長い期間成功するためには何が必要か、あなたの意見を述べてください。
> In your opinion, what is required to have long-term success for a celebrity in Japan?

❖ 答えよう

A1 Who is your favorite celebrity in Japan?
北野武です。// 大泉洋です。
Takeshi Kitano. // Yo Oizumi.

A2 Could you describe the personality of your favorite Japanese celebrity?
私の好きな有名人は明石家さんまです。彼はかなり頭がよくて、面白いです。
My favorite celebrity is Sanma Akashiya. He is quite smart and funny.

B1 In your opinion, what is required to have long-term success for a celebrity in Japan?
①私の意見では、有名人として長い期間成功するためには、マルチな才能が必要です。
In my opinion, to have long-term success as a celebrity is to have multiple talents.

②日本の有名人を見てみると、多くの有名人がショーでMCをしたり、歌ったり、映画で上手に演技さえできます。
If you take a look at celebrities in Japan, a lot of them can host a variety show, sing and even act well in movies.

③私は日本で有名人として長い間成功するのはかなり大変だと思います。
I think it is quite difficult to have long-term success as a celebrity in Japan.

❖ 練習しよう：❶ 単語ごとに英訳しよう
　　　　　　❷「／」ごとに英訳しよう

B1 In your opinion, what is required to have long-term success for a celebrity in Japan?

①に　私の　意見　／持つこと　長い期間　成功　／として　1つの　有名人
In my opinion, / to have long-term success / as a celebrity

／だ　持つこと　マルチな　才能。
/ is to have multiple talents.

②もし　あなた　見てみる　有名人　／に　日本　／たくさんの　彼ら
If you take a look at celebrities / in Japan, / a lot of them

／できる　ホストする　1つの　バラエティーショー　／歌う
/ can host a variety show, / sing

／そして　さえ　演技する　うまく　／に　映画。
/ and even act well / in movies.

③私　思う　／それ　だ　すっかり　難しい　／持つこと　長い間　成功
I think / it is quite difficult / to have long-term success

／として　1人の　有名人　／に　日本。
/ as a celebrity / in Japan.

❖ 覚えよう

B1 **In your opinion, what is required to have long-term success for a celebrity in Japan?**

In my opinion, to have long-term success as a celebrity is to have multiple talents. If you take a look at celebrities in Japan, a lot of them can host a variety show, sing and even act well in movies. I think it is quite difficult to have long-term success as a celebrity in Japan.

❖ 話してみよう

> **A1** Would you like to be an actor?
> **A2** Could you explain why you prefer either Japanese or foreign movies?
> **B1** What are some reasons that celebrities suddenly become less popular?

59 Telecommunications
通信

❖ 質問しよう

A1 あなたはどんな種類の携帯電話を使っていますか。
What kind of cellphone do you use?

A2 あなたは1日に何通ぐらいメールを送りますか。
How many text messages do you write on average per day?

B1 あなたの携帯電話の一番好きな機能は何ですか。
Would you describe the most useful features of your cellphone?

❖ 答えよう

A1 What kind of cell phone do you use?
スマートフォンです。
A smartphone.

A2 How many text messages do you write on average per day?
私は1日にテキスト・メッセージを約30通送ります。私のテキスト・メッセージは普段はとても短いですが。
I send about thirty text messages per day. My text messages are usually very short, though.

B1 Would you describe the most useful features of your cellphone?
①私はスマートフォンを使っています。
I use a smartphone.

②私が最も好きな機能はアプリをダウンロードできることです。
The feature I like most is being able to download apps.

③これによって自分の電話をカスタマイズできます。
This allows me to customize my phone.

④例えば、私は、ソーシャルネットワーク、ゲーム、語学学習のためのアプリをダウンロードしました。

For example, I have downloaded apps for social networking, games, and language learning.

⑤私のお気に入りは、写真編集のためのものです。

My favorite one is for photo editing.

⑥それを使えば、様々な創造的な方法で、自分個人の写真を作ることができます。

It allows me to personalize my pictures in many creative ways.

❖ 練習しよう：❶ 単語ごとに英訳しよう
　　　　　　　❷「／」ごとに英訳しよう

B1 Would you describe the most useful features of your cellphone?

①私　使う　1つの　スマートフォン。

I use a smartphone.

②その　特徴　私　好きだ　最も

The feature I like most

／だ　できること　ダウンロードする　アプリ。

/ is being able to download apps.

③これ　許す　私　／カスタマイズすること　私の　電話。

This allows me / to customize my phone.

④例えば、／私　持つ　ダウンロードした　アプリ

For example, / I have downloaded apps

／ための　ソーシャルネットワーキング　／ゲーム　／そして　言語　学習。

/ for social networking, / games, / and language learning.

⑤私の　お気に入りの　1つ　だ　／ための　写真　編集。

My favorite one is / for photo editing.

⑥それ　許す　私　／に　個人化する　私の　写真

It allows me / to personalize my pictures

/に 多くの クリエイティブな 方法。
/ in many creative ways.

❖ 覚えよう

B1 **Would you describe the most useful features of your cellphone?**

I use a smartphone. The feature I like most is being able to download apps. This allows me to customize my phone. For example, I have downloaded apps for social networking, games, and language learning. My favorite one is for photo editing. It allows me to personalize my pictures in many creative ways.

❖ 話してみよう

> **A1** When did you get your first cellphone?
> **A2** What is a good age for a young person to get a cellphone?
> **B1** Could you try to describe how cellphones will change in the future?

60 Computers
コンピュータ

❖ 質問しよう

> **A1** あなたは毎日どのくらいの時間コンピュータを使いますか。
> How much time do you spend on the computer every day?
>
> **A2** あなたは、コンピュータで何をすることが好きですか。
> What's your favorite thing to do on a computer?
>
> **B1** もしコンピュータを使うのをやめたら、あなたの生活はどう変化しますか。
> How would your life change if you stopped using computers?

❖ 答えよう

A1 How much time do you spend on the computer every day?
約1時間です。//3時間か4時間です。
About an hour. // Three or four hours.

A2 What's your favorite thing to do on a computer?
私は新しいことを学ぶのが好きなので、記事を読んだり、ビデオを見たりすることにたくさん時間を使います。
I enjoy learning new things, so I spend a lot of time reading articles or watching videos.

B1 How would your life change if you stopped using computers?
①子供のころから使っているので、コンピュータなしの生活を想像することは難しいです。

It's hard to imagine my life without computers because I've been using them since I was a child.

②しかし祖母はコンピュータを使わないので、たぶん私の生活も祖母のようになるでしょう。

But my grandmother doesn't use computers, so maybe my life would be like hers.

③彼女は、小説や雑誌などを私よりもたくさん読みます。
She reads more than I do—like novels and magazines.

④彼女はEメールを使わないので、たくさん手紙や葉書を書きます。
She doesn't use email, so she writes a lot of letters and postcards.

⑤だから私もたぶん同じことをすると思います。
So maybe I would do those things, too.

⑥そしてたぶんコンピュータを持たなければ、時間を浪費しないでしょう。
And maybe I wouldn't waste so much time if I didn't have a computer.

❖ 練習しよう：❶ 単語ごとに英訳しよう
　　　　　　　❷「／」ごとに英訳しよう

B1 How would your life change if you stopped using computers?

①それだ　困難　想像すること　／私の　生活　なし　コンピュータ
It's hard to imagine / my life without computers

／なぜなら／私持つ　だった　使っている　それら
/ because / I've been using them

／以来　私　だった　1つの　子供。
/ since I was a child.

②しかし　／私の　祖母　ない　使う　コンピュータ
But / my grandmother doesn't use computers,

／だから　たぶん／私の　生活　だろう　だ　のよう　彼女のもの。
/ so maybe / my life would be like hers.

③彼女　読む　より多く　／よりも　私　する
She reads more / than I do

／のような　小説　そして　雑誌。
/ —like novels and magazines.

④彼女 ない 使う Eメール /だから /彼女 書く たくさんの 手紙
She doesn't use email, / so / she writes a lot of letters

/そして 葉書。
/ and postcards.

⑤だから /たぶん 私 だろう する /それらの こと も。
So / maybe I would do / those things, too.

⑥そして たぶん /私 ないだろう 無駄にする
And maybe / I wouldn't waste

/そんなに 多くの 時間
/ so much time

/もし 私 なかった 持つ 1つの コンピュータ。
/ if I didn't have a computer.

❖ 覚えよう

B1 **How would your life change if you stopped using computers?**

It's hard to imagine my life without computers because I've been using them since I was a child. But my grandmother doesn't use computers, so maybe my life would be like hers. She reads more than I do—like novels and magazines. She doesn't use email, so she writes a lot of letters and postcards. So maybe I would do those things, too. And maybe I wouldn't waste so much time if I didn't have a computer.

❖ 話してみよう

A1 Do you have a computer at home?

A2 What is the most useful software program on your computer?

B1 What are some of the negative effects of the widespread use of home computers?

61 Shopping & Family Finance
買い物・家計

❖ 質問しよう

A1 あなたは毎月お小遣いをいくらもらっていますか。
How much spending money do you get every month?

A2 あなたは毎月のお小遣いをどうやって得ていますか。
How do you get your monthly spending money?

B1 あなたのお小遣いを普段どう使っているのか説明してください。
Could you tell me how you usually use your spending money?

❖ 答えよう

A1 How much spending money do you get every month?
約3万円です。
About thirty thousand yen.

A2 How do you get your monthly spending money?
私はカフェでアルバイトしています。// 両親から毎月お金をもらいます。
I have a part-time job at a cafe. // My parents give me money every month.

B1 Could you tell me how you usually use your spending money?

①私は主に楽しいことをするために使います。
I mainly spend money on things that are fun.

②私は学校や仕事で忙しいので、友達とリラックスする時間を持つことは私にとって重要です。
I'm busy with school and work, so it's important for me to have time to relax with my friends.

③私は外食したり、映画を見たり、あるいはカラオケをすることが好きです。
I like going out to eat, watching movies or going to karaoke.

④また、買い物も大好きです。でも、お金を簡単に使いすぎるので、そうたびたびは行きません。
I also love to go shopping, but it's too easy to spend a lot of money, so I don't go so often.

❖ 練習しよう：❶ 単語ごとに英訳しよう
　　　　　　❷「／」ごとに英訳しよう

B1 Could you tell me how you usually use your spending money?

①私　主に　費やす　お金　／に　物　／それ　だ　楽しい。
I mainly spend money / on things / that are fun.

②私だ　忙しい　／で　学校　そして　仕事　／だから
I'm busy / with school and work, / so

／それだ　重要　にとって　私　／持つこと　時間
/ it's important for me / to have time

／ための　リラックスする　と一緒に　私の　友達。
/ to relax with my friends.

③私　好きだ　出かけること　ために　食べる　／見ること　映画
I like going out to eat, / watching movies

／または　行くこと　に　カラオケ。
/ or going to karaoke.

④私　また　愛する　／行くこと　買い物　／しかし
I also love / to go shopping, / but

／それだ　あまりに　簡単　／費やすこと　たくさんの　お金
/ it's too easy / to spend a lot of money,

／だから　／私　ない　行く　／そんなに　しばしば。
/ so / I don't go / so often.

❖ 覚えよう

B1 **Could you tell me how you usually use your spending money?**

I mainly spend money on things that are fun. I'm busy with school and work, so it's important for me to have time to relax with my friends. I like going out to eat, watching movies or going to karaoke. I also love to go shopping, but it's too easy to spend a lot of money, so I don't go so often.

❖ 話してみよう

> **A1** What is the name of your favorite convenience store?
> **A2** What do you usually buy at convenience stores?
> **B1** Could you describe the difference between supermarkets and convenience stores?

62 Work
労働

❖ 質問しよう

A1 あなたはアルバイトをしていますか。
Do you have a part-time job?

A2 大学生の間で一般的なアルバイトは何ですか。
What are some common part-time jobs held by university students?

B1 今までしたアルバイトでどんな業務を担ったことがありますか。
Could you describe the responsibilities of a part-time job you had?

❖ 答えよう

A1 **Do you have a part-time job?**
はい。// いいえ。// はい、しています。// いいえ、していません。
Yes. // No. // Yes, I do. // No, I don't.

A2 **What are some common part-time jobs held by university students?**
多くの大学生はレストランかカフェで働いています。
Many university students work at restaurants or cafes.

B1 **Could you describe the responsibilities of a part-time job you had?**

①私はレストランで働いていた時、たくさんの業務を抱えていました。
When I worked at a restaurant, I had a lot of responsibilities.

②最初は覚えるのが大変でしたが、少しずつ楽になりました。
It was hard to remember everything at first, but it got easier.

③私はお冷やメニューをお客さんに出す仕事をしていました。
I gave customers water and menus.

④メニューの内容を説明して、注文もとりました。
I described items on the menu, and I took their orders.

⑤でも、一番大変だったことはお客さんの特別なリクエストに応えることでした。
But the hardest part was trying to help customers with special requests.

⑥例えば、音楽がうるさすぎるとか、食事が冷たいと言う人がいました。
For example, some people said the music was too loud, or their food was cold.

⑦でも私は常に皆がハッピーになれるように最善を尽くしました。
But I always did my best to help everyone.

❖ 練習しよう：❶ 単語ごとに英訳しよう
　　　　　　　❷「/」ごとに英訳しよう

B1 **Could you describe the responsibilities of a part-time job you had?**

①時　私　働いた　で　1つの　レストラン
When I worked at a restaurant,

/私は　持った　たくさんの　責任。
/ I had a lot of responsibilities.

②それ　だった　困難　/覚えること　すべてのこと　最初は
It was hard / to remember everything at first,

/しかし　/それ　なった　より簡単に。
/ but / it got easier.

③私　与えた　客　/水　そして　メニュー。
I gave customers / water and menus.

④私　描写した　アイテム　/に　その　メニュー
I described items / on the menu,

/そして　私　とった　彼らの　オーダー。
/ and I took their orders.

⑤しかし　その　最も困難　部分　だった
But / the hardest part was

/トライすること　助けること　客　/と一緒に　特別な　リクエスト。
/ trying to help customers / with special requests.

⑥例えば　/何人かの　人々　言った
For example, / some people said

/その　音楽　だった　あまりに　大きい
/ the music was too loud,

/または　彼らの　食べ物　だった　冷たい。
/ or their food was cold.

⑦しかし　/私　いつも　した　私の　ベスト　/ために　助ける　みな。
But / I always did my best / to help everyone.

❖ 覚えよう

B1 **Could you describe the responsibilities of a part-time job you had?**

When I worked at a restaurant, I had a lot of responsibilities. It was hard to remember everything at first, but it got easier. I gave customers water and menus. I described items on the menu, and I took their orders. But the hardest part was trying to help customers with special requests. For example, some people said the music was too loud, or their food was cold. But I always did my best to help everyone.

❖ 話してみよう

A1 Do most of your friends have part-time jobs?

A2 What kind of job do you want to get after graduation?

B1 How are you going to maintain a healthy work-life balance in the future?

63 Job Hunting
就職活動

❖ 質問しよう

A1「ジョブ・ハンティング」は日本語で何と言いますか。
How do you say "job hunting" in Japanese?

A2 あなたはいつ就職活動を始めるつもりですか。
When are you going to begin job hunting?

B1 あなたが働く理想的な会社について話してください。
Could you describe an ideal company to work for?

❖ 答えよう

A1 How do you say "job hunting" in Japanese?
就職活動です。// 就活です。
Shushoku katsudou. // Shukatsu.

A2 When are you going to begin job hunting?
私は3年生になったら始めるつもりです。// 私は3年生の終わりに始めるつもりです。

I'm going to start when I'm in my third year. // I'll start at the end of my third year.

B1 Could you describe an ideal company to work for?
①私にとって重要なことは、その会社が従業員に対して感謝を見せるかどうかということです。

For me, the most important thing is for the company to show appreciation to its employees.

②従業員がいなくては、会社は存在しないので、私は会社を経営する人々はそれを適切に認めるべきだと思います。

Without the employees, there would be no company, and I think the people who run the company should acknowledge that.

③これを実現する方法はいくらでもあります。
　There are many ways that companies can do this.
④例えば、従業員が無料で食事をとれるカフェテリアを持っている企業があります。
　For example, some companies have cafeterias where employees can eat for free.
⑤また無料のジム会員権を従業員に渡している企業もあります。
　Other companies give employees free gym memberships.
⑥これらのようなことが、従業員を幸せにし、忠実にさせます。
　Things like these can make employees happy and loyal.

❖ 練習しよう：❶ 単語ごとに英訳しよう　❷「/」ごとに英訳しよう

B1 Could you describe an ideal company to work for?

①にとって　私　/その　最も　重要な　こと　だ
　For me, / the most important thing is

/にとって　その　会社　/見せること　感謝
　/ for the company / to show appreciation

/に　それの　従業員。
　/ to its employees.

②なしで　その　従業員　/そこに　だろう　ある　ない　会社
　Without the employees, / there would be no company,

/そして　/私　思う　/その　人々　/彼　走らす　その　会社
　/ and / I think / the people / who run the company

/べき　認める　それ。
　/ should acknowledge that.

③そこに　ある　たくさんの　方法　/という　会社　できる　する　これ。
　There are many ways / that companies can do this.

④例えば　/いくつかの　会社　持つ　カフェテリア
　For example, / some companies have cafeterias

/ そこ 従業員 できる 食べる /無料で。
/ where employees can eat / for free.

⑤他の 会社 与える 従業員 /無料の ジム メンバーシップ。
Other companies give employees / free gym memberships.

⑥こと のような これら /できる させる 従業員
Things like these / can make employees

/ 幸せ そして 忠実。
/ happy and loyal.

❖ 覚えよう

B1 **Could you describe an ideal company to work for?**

For me, the most important thing is for the company to show appreciation to its employees. Without the employees, there would be no company, and I think the people who run the company should acknowledge that. There are many ways that companies can do this. For example, some companies have cafeterias where employees can eat for free. Other companies give employees free gym memberships. Things like these can make employees happy and loyal.

❖ 話してみよう

A1 Are you looking forward to job hunting?

A2 Could you describe your current feelings about job hunting?

B1 What changes would you like to see in the job hunting system in Japan?

64 Business
ビジネス

❖ 質問しよう

> **A1** あなたは起業したいと思いますか。
> Would you like to start your own business?
>
> **A2** もしあなたが起業したら、どんな会社を作りますか。
> If you started your own company, what kind of company would it be?
>
> **B1** もしあなたが起業したら、どんな職場環境を作りたいですか。
> If you started your own company, what kind of work environment would you want to create?

❖ 答えよう

A1 Would you like to start your own business?
はい。// いいえ。// はい、思います。// いいえ、思いません。
Yes. // No. // Yes, I would. // No, I wouldn't.

A2 If you started your own company, what kind of company would it be?
私はウェディング・プランニングの会社を作りたいと思います。
I would like to make a wedding planning company.

B1 If you started your own company, what kind of work environment would you want to create?

①もし私が起業したら、従業員に私は彼らの判断やアイディアを大切にすると伝えます。

If I started my own company, I would like to show my employees that I respect their judgment and ideas.

②例えば、私は従業員に自分の労働時間を選ばせます。

For example, I would let employees choose their own work hours.

③朝早く来て日中早く帰る社員もいれば、昼食後出社して夜遅くまで残ることを選ぶ社員もいるかもしれません。

Some people would come early in the morning and leave earlier in the day, but others might choose to come after lunch and stay much later into the evening.

④もしよい仕事をしているなら、私は自分の管理は自分でさせようと思います。

If they are doing good work, I'd like to let them manage themselves.

❖ 練習しよう：❶ 単語ごとに英訳しよう
　　　　　　 ❷「／」ごとに英訳しよう

B1 **If you started your own company, what kind of work environment would you want to create?**

①もし　私　スタートした　私の　自分の　会社　／私　したい　見せる
If I started my own company, / I would like to show

／私の　従業員　／ということ　私　尊敬する　彼らの　判断
/ my employees / that I respect their judgment

／そして　アイディア。
/ and ideas.

②例えば　／私　だろう　させる　従業員　選ぶ
For example, / I would let employees choose

／彼らの　自分の　働く　時間。
/ their own work hours.

③何人かの　人々　だろう　来る　／早く　に　その　朝
Some people would come / early in the morning

／そして　離れる　より早く　に　その　日　／しかし
/ and leave earlier in the day, / but

／他の人たち　かもしれなかった　選ぶ　／来ること　の後　昼食
/ others might choose / to come after lunch

/ そして 滞在する ずっと より遅く / の中に その 夕方。
/ and stay much later / into the evening.

④もし 彼ら だ している よい 仕事 / 私したい させる 彼ら
If they are doing good work, / I'd like to let them

/ 管理する 彼ら自身。
/ manage themselves.

❖ 覚えよう

B1 **If you started your own company, what kind of work environment would you want to create?**

If I started my own company, I would like to show my employees that I respect their judgment and ideas. For example, I would let employees choose their own work hours. Some people would come early in the morning and leave earlier in the day, but others might choose to come after lunch and stay much later into the evening. If they are doing good work, I'd like to let them manage themselves.

❖ 話してみよう

> **A1** Do you read the business section of the newspaper?
> **A2** Could you talk about a company that you like?
> **B1** What is necessary to be a successful CEO?

65 Stocks
株

❖ 質問しよう

> **A1** あなたは 株式投資に興味がありますか。
> Are you interested in equity investments?
>
> **A2** どうして株式に興味を持ったのですか。
> How did you become interested in stocks?
>
> **B1** 今1千万円投資できるとしたら、あなたはどうしますか。
> If you had ten million yen to invest right now, what would you do?

❖ 答えよう

A1 **Are you interested in equity investments?**
はい。// いいえ。// はい、あります。// いいえ、ありません。
Yes. // No. // Yes, I am. // No, I'm not.

A2 **How did you become interested in stocks?**
私の父が長い間株に投資していて、それで私も興味を持つようになりました。
My father has been investing in stocks for a long time, and that's how I got interested.

B1 **If you had ten million yen to invest right now, what would you do?**

①もし今1千万円投資できたら、私はいくつか異なる方法で投資すると思います。
If I had ten million yen to invest right now, I would invest in several different ways.

②投資する時は多角的に行うことが重要です。
It's important to diversify when investing.

③基本的にすべてのお金を1つの銘柄に投資するべきではありません。
Basically, this means you should not put all of your money into a single kind of investment.

④私だったらいくらかを大企業に、またいくらかを中小企業に投資します。
I would invest in some large companies and some small ones.

⑤国内と海外の両方の企業に投資します。
I'd put some money in both domestic and foreign companies.

⑥また、いくらかを貴金属にも投資します。
I'd also put some money in precious metals.

❖ 練習しよう：❶ 単語ごとに英訳しよう
　　　　　　 ❷ 「／」ごとに英訳しよう

B1 If you had ten million yen to invest right now, what would you do?

①もし　私が　持った　1千万　円　/ため　投資する　ただちに　今
If I had ten million yen / to invest right now,

/私　だろう　投資する　/に　いくつかの　異なった　方法。
/ I would invest / in several different ways.

②それだ　重要　/多様にすること　/時　投資している。
It's important / to diversify / when investing.

③基本的に　/これ　意味する　/あなた　べき　ない　置く
Basically, / this means / you should not put

/すべて　の　あなたの　お金
/ all of your money

/の中に　1つの　単一の　種類　の　投資。
/ into a single kind of investment.

④私　だろう　投資する　/に　いくつかの　広い　会社
I would invest / in some large companies

/そして　いくつかの　小さい　1つ。
/ and some small ones.

⑤私だろう　置く　いくつかの　お金　/に　両方
I'd put some money / in both

/国内の　そして　外国の　会社。
/ domestic and foreign companies.

⑥私だろう　また　置く　いくらかの　お金　/に　貴重な　金属。
I'd also put some money / in precious metals.

❖ 覚えよう

B1 **If you had ten million yen to invest right now, what would you do?**

If I had ten million yen to invest right now, I would invest in several different ways. It's important to diversify when investing. Basically, this means you should not put all of your money into a single kind of investment. I would invest in some large companies and some small ones. I'd put some money in both domestic and foreign companies. I'd also put some money in precious metals.

❖ 話してみよう

A1 Do you invest in stocks?
A2 What are some companies that have valuable stock?
B1 Could you describe the basic points of how the stock market works?

66 Economy & Finance
経済・財政・金融

❖ 質問しよう

> **A1** 今までに「公定歩合」という言葉を聞いたことがありますか。
> Have you heard the term "official discount rate"?
>
> **A2** 公定歩合とは何ですか。
> What is the official discount rate?
>
> **B1** 公定歩合の機能を説明してもらえますか。
> Could you explain the function of the official discount rate?

❖ 答えよう

A1 Have you heard the term "official discount rate"?
はい。// いいえ。// はい、あります。// いいえ、ありません。// まったく。// たぶん。
Yes. // No. // Yes, I have. // No, I haven't. // Never. // Maybe.

A2 What is the official discount rate?
公定歩合とは中央銀行が地方銀行に融資する際に適応する利子のことです。
That is the interest rate that the central bank applies to private banks when the central bank gives loans to the private banks.

B1 Could you explain the function of the official discount rate?
①不景気の際には、中央銀行は通常公定歩合を引き下げます。
The central bank usually lowers the official discount rate when the economy slows down.

②公定歩合を引き下げると、企業の財政負担が軽減されます。
Lowering the official discount rate will lower the financial burden on businesses.

③それによって個人投資の需要が刺激され、経済の発展につながります。

It stimulates the demand for private funds, which leads to a more prosperous economy.

④一方、経済があまりに急速に成長した時には、中央銀行は公定歩合を引き下げ、それによって経済活動が減速します。

On the other hand, when the economy grows too rapidly, the central bank raises the rate, which slows down business activity.

⑤経済のバランスを保たせることが、公定歩合の主な機能です。

Keeping the economy in balance is the main function of the official discount rate.

❖ 練習しよう：❶ 単語ごとに英訳しよう
　　　　　　❷「／」ごとに英訳しよう

B1 Could you explain the function of the official discount rate?

①その　中央銀行　普段　下げる　／その　公定歩合

The central bank usually lowers / the official discount rate

／時　その　経済　スローダウンする。

/ when the economy slows down.

②下げること　その　公定歩合　／だろう　下げる　その　財政の　負担

Lowering the official discount rate / will lower the financial burden

／に　ビジネス。

/ on businesses.

③それは　刺激する　その　需要　／ための　個人ファンド　／それ　導く

It stimulates the demand / for private funds, / which leads

／に　1つの　より　繁栄した　経済。

/ to a more prosperous economy.

④その一方で　／時　その　経済　成長する　／あまりに　急速に

On the other hand, / when the economy grows / too rapidly,

/ その　中央銀行　/ 上げる　その　レート　/ それ　スローダウンする
/ the central bank /raises the rate, /which slows down

/ ビジネス　活動。
/ business activity.

⑤保つこと　その　経済　/ に　バランス　/ だ　その　主要な　機能
Keeping the economy / in balance / is the main function

/ の　その　公定歩合。
/ of the official discount rate.

❖ 覚えよう

B1 **Could you explain the function of the official discount rate?**

The central bank usually lowers the official discount rate when the economy slows down. Lowering the official discount rate will lower the financial burden on businesses. It stimulates the demand for private funds, which leads to a more prosperous economy. On the other hand, when the economy grows too rapidly, the central bank raises the rate, which slows down business activity. Keeping the economy in balance is the main function of the official discount rate.

❖ 話してみよう

A1 Do you read news articles about the economy?

A2 What is the current state of the Japanese economy?

B1 What would be one way to improve the Japanese economy?

67 International Finance
国際経済・金融

❖ 質問しよう

A1 今までに外国の通貨を使ったことがありますか。
Have you ever used foreign money?

A2 現在の日本円とアメリカ・ドルの為替レートはいくらですか。
What is the current exchange rate between the Japanese yen and the US dollar?

B1 円高の利点を1つ挙げてください。
Would you describe one of the benefits of a strong Japanese yen?

❖ 答えよう

A1 **Have you ever used foreign money?**
はい。// いいえ。// はい、あります。// いいえ、ありません。// 何度も。// 一度も。
Yes. // No. // Yes, I have. // No, I haven't. // Many times. // Never.

A2 **What is the current exchange rate between the Japanese yen and the US dollar?**
今現在1ドル約120円です。
It's about one hundred and twenty yen to the dollar right now.

B1 **Would you describe one of the benefits of a strong Japanese yen?**
①日本に住み、働いている人にとっては、円高は、例えば、アメリカに行く時により高い購買力を発揮します。

For someone living and working in Japan, a strong yen means that they have more buying power when they go, for example, to the United States.

②これは、日本人旅行者にとってはよい点です。
This is a good thing for Japanese tourists.

③しかしながら、日本企業にとっては、円高は常によいとは限りません。というのは、輸出相手国の購買力が下がり、売上に響くからです。
For Japanese companies, though, a strong yen is not always good because the countries they export to have less buying power, and this hurts sales.

❖ 練習しよう：❶ 単語ごとに英訳しよう
❷「 / 」ごとに英訳しよう

B1 Would you describe one of the benefits of a strong Japanese yen?

①にとって 誰か /住んでいる そして 働いている に 日本
For someone / living and working in Japan,

/1つの 強い 円 意味する
/ a strong yen means

/ということ 彼らは 持つ より多くの 買うこと 力
/ that they have more buying power

/時 彼ら 行く /例えば /に その 合衆国。
/ when they go, / for example, / to the United States.

②これ だ 1つの よい こと /にとって 日本人 旅行者。
This is a good thing /for Japanese tourists.

③にとって 日本の 会社 /けれども
For Japanese companies, / though,

/1つの 強い 円 だ ない いつも よい /なぜなら
/ a strong yen / is not always good / because

/その 国々 彼ら 輸出する に /持つ より少ない 買うこと 力
/ the countries they export to / have less buying power,

/そして これ 傷つける 売上。
/ and this hurts sales.

❖ 覚えよう

B1 **Would you describe one of the benefits of a strong Japanese yen?**

For someone living and working in Japan, a strong yen means that they have more buying power when they go, for example, to the United States. This is a good thing for Japanese tourists. For Japanese companies, though, a strong yen is not always good because the countries they export to have less buying power, and this hurts sales.

❖ 話してみよう

> **A1** Is the Japanese yen strong or weak now?
>
> **A2** Who benefits if the Japanese yen is weak?
>
> **B1** Could you describe how the Japanese yen becomes stronger or weaker?

68 Taxes
税

❖ 質問しよう

> **A1** 消費税が上がったのを知っていますか。
> Did you know that the sales tax has risen?
>
> **A2** 現在の消費税は何パーセントですか。
> What percent is the sales tax now?
>
> **B1** 消費増税の利点を挙げてください。
> Could you explain the advantages of raising the sales tax?

❖ 答えよう

A1 Did you know that the sales tax has risen?
はい。// いいえ。// 本当ですか。
Yes. // No. // Really?

A2 What percent is the sales tax now?
現在8パーセントです。
It is eight percent now.

B1 Could you explain the advantages of raising the sales tax?

①ほとんどの消費者が消費税の引き上げに不平を言い、支出を抑えたとしても、国にとってはいくつか重要なメリットがあります。

Even though most consumers complain about increases in the sales tax and may cut back on their spending, there are some important benefits for the country.

②消費税率の引き上げによって国家予算が増え、それが多くのポジティブな影響を及ぼします。

Raising the sales tax rate boosts the national budget, which has a number of positive effects.

③例えば 社会保障がより安定します。

For example, it makes the social security system more stable.

④また国の自然災害からの復興にも役立ちます。
It also helps the country to recover from natural disasters.

❖ 練習しよう：❶ 単語ごとに英訳しよう
　　　　　　❷「/」ごとに英訳しよう

B1 Could you explain the advantages of raising the sales tax?

①たとえ〜けれども　/ほとんどの　消費者　不平を言う
Even though / most consumers complain

/について　増加　/に　その　消費税
/ about increases / in the sales tax,

/そして　かもしれない　減らす　/の上に　彼らの　支出
/ and may cut back / on their spending,

/そこに　ある　いくつかの　重要な　利点　/にとって　その　国。
/ there are some important benefits / for the country.

②上げること　その　消費税　割合　/押し上げる　その　国の　予算
Raising the sales tax rate / boosts the national budget,

/それ　持つ　多数の　ポジティブな　効果。
/ which has a number of positive effects.

③例えば　/それ　作る　その　社会　保障　システム　/より　安定。
For example, / it makes the social security system / more stable.

④それ　また　助ける　その　国　/回復すること　/から　自然　災害。
It also helps the country / to recover / from natural disasters.

❖ 覚えよう

B1 Could you explain the advantages of raising the sales tax?

Even though most consumers complain about increases in the sales tax and may cut back on their spending, there are some important benefits for the country. Raising the sales tax rate boosts the national budget, which has a number of positive effects. For example, it makes the social security system more stable. It also helps the country to recover from natural disasters.

❖ 話してみよう

> **A1** Would you like the sales tax to be lower?
> **A2** Can you name a few different kinds of taxes?
> **B1** Could you explain why people are required to pay income tax?

69 Industry in General
工業一般

❖ 質問しよう

A1 今までに「産業革命」という言葉を聞いたことがありますか。
Have you heard the term "Industrial Revolution"?

A2 産業革命について知っていることを話してください。
What do you know about the Industrial Revolution?

B1 機械の利用は世界史にどのような影響を与えましたか。
How did the use of machines affect world history?

❖ 答えよう

A1 Have you heard the term "Industrial Revolution"?
はい。// いいえ。// はい、あります。// それは何ですか。
Yes. // No. // Yes, I have. // What's that?

A2 What do you know about the Industrial Revolution?
産業革命は、工場をベースに産業が導入された18世紀の中ごろを指します。

The Industrial Revolution was the period in the middle of the 18th century when factory-based industry was introduced.

B1 How did the use of machines affect world history?
①機械の出現は世界史に非常に、大きな影響を与えました。それは多くはプラスでしたが、いくつかマイナスの影響もありました。

The advent of machines had a great impact on world history, mostly positive and some negative.

②プラスの点は、機械の利用によって生産性が向上し、その結果平均収入が上昇し、人口が増えたことです。

The positive points are that the use of mechanized machines raised production levels with the result that the average income went up and the population grew.

③ただプラスだけではありませんでした。工場は製造需要に追いつくため、より多くの労働力が必要でした。それは子供でさえ危険な状況で強制的に働かされるほどでした。

It wasn't all positive, however: factories needed more labor to keep up with production demand, so much so that even young children were forced to work in dangerous conditions.

❖ 練習しよう：❶ 単語ごとに英訳しよう
   ❷「／」ごとに英訳しよう

B1 How did the use of machines affect world history?

① その　出現　の　機械　／持った　1つの　偉大な　インパクト
　The advent of machines / had a great impact

／に　世界の　歴史　／ほとんど　ポジティブ
／ on world history, / mostly positive

／そして　いくつか　ネガティブ。
／ and some negative.

② その　ポジティブな　ポイント　だ　／ということ　その　使用
　The positive points are / that the use

／の　機械化される　機械　／上昇した　製造　レベル
／ of mechanized machines / raised production levels

／と一緒に　その　結果　／という　その　平均　収入　行く　上に
／ with the result / that the average income went up

／そして　その　人口　育った。
／ and the population grew.

③ それ　でなかった　すべて　ポジティブ　／しかしながら
　It wasn't all positive, / however:

／工場　必要だった　より多くの　労働
／ factories needed more labor

／ため　ついていく　製造　需要　／非常にそうなので
／ to keep up with production demand, / so much so that

/ さえ 若い 子供たち だった 強制された / 働くこと
/ even young children were forced / to work

/ に 危険な 状況。
/ in dangerous conditions.

❖ 覚えよう

B1 **How did the use of machines affect world history?**

The advent of machines had a great impact on world history, mostly positive and some negative. The positive points are that the use of mechanized machines raised production levels with the result that the average income went up and the population grew. It wasn't all positive, however: factories needed more labor to keep up with production demand, so much so that even young children were forced to work in dangerous conditions.

❖ 話してみよう

A1 What is one product that is manufactured in Japan?
A2 Can you give a definition of industry?
B1 How have robotics changed the way things are manufactured?

70 The Automobile Industry
自動車産業

❖ 質問しよう

A1 あなたは自動車会社で働きたいと思いますか。
Would you like to work for an automobile company?

A2 トヨタが日本で最も売れている自動車メーカーであるのはどうしてだと思いますか。
Why do you think Toyota is the top-selling car brand in Japan?

B1 車のタイプを1種類挙げて、その顧客層を説明してください。
Could you choose a car model and describe its target market?

❖ 答えよう

A1 Would you like to work for an automobile company?
はい。// いいえ。// はい、働きたいです。// いいえ、働きたくありません。// あまり。
Yes. // No. // Yes, I would. // No, I wouldn't. // Not really.

A2 Why do you think Toyota is the top-selling car brand in Japan?
その理由の1つは、トヨタがジャストインタイム生産方式を実践したからです。
One of the reasons is because they implemented the just-in-time production system.

B1 Could you choose a car model and describe its target market?

①具体的にどの車種ということはできないのですが、ハイブリッドカーは、二酸化炭素の排出量を減らすことによって、環境をよくしたいと思う人たちに人気があります。

I can't specify a particular model, but hybrid cars appeal to people who want to help the environment by reducing carbon emissions.

②ハイブリッドカーは、従来の自動車より、はるかに燃費がいいです。

They use much less gasoline than conventional cars.

③ハイブリッドカーの人気の理由は、もう1つあります。

There's another reason hybrid cars are popular.

④ハイブリッドカーは燃費がいいので、維持費が安く済みます。

Because they use less gas, they cost less to operate.

⑤このように、ハイブリッドカーは経済性を求める人々の間でも人気があります。

This makes hybrid cars popular among people who like to save money, too.

❖ 練習しよう：❶ 単語ごとに英訳しよう
　　　　　　　　❷「 / 」ごとに英訳しよう

B1 Could you choose a car model and describe its target market?

①私　できない　特定する　/1つの　特定の　モデル　/しかし
I can't specify / a particular model, / but

/ハイブリッドカー　訴える　/に　人々　/彼ら　ほしい　助けること
/ hybrid cars appeal / to people / who want to help

/その　環境　/によって　減らす　二酸化炭素　排出。
/ the environment / by reducing carbon emissions.

②それら　使う　はるかに　より少ない　ガソリン　/よりも　従来の　車。
They use much less gasoline / than conventional cars.

③そこにある　もう1つの　理由　/ ハイブリッドカー　だ　人気がある。
There's another reason / hybrid cars are popular.

④なぜなら　それら　使う　より少ない　ガソリン
/ Because they use less gas,

/ それら　かかる　より少ない　/ ため　作動する。
/ they cost less / to operate.

⑤これ　させる　ハイブリッドカー　人気がある　/ の間で　人々
This makes hybrid cars popular / among people

/ 彼ら　好きだ　節約すること　お金　/ も。
/ who like to save money, too.

❖ 覚えよう

B1 Could you choose a car model and describe its target market?

I can't specify a particular model, but hybrid cars appeal to people who want to help the environment by reducing carbon emissions. They use much less gasoline than conventional cars. There's another reason hybrid cars are popular. Because they use less gas, they cost less to operate. This makes hybrid cars popular among people who like to save money, too.

❖ 話してみよう

A1 What is your favorite carmaker?

A2 Could you describe a TV commercial for a car that you like?

B1 In your opinion, how will the automobile industry change in the next twenty years?

71 Heavy Industry
重工業

❖ 質問しよう

> **A1** 今まで造船所を訪れたことがありますか。
> Have you ever visited a shipyard?
>
> **A2** 日本の中で製造業で知られている地域をいくつか教えてください。
> What are some parts of Japan known for manufacturing?
>
> **B1** 「重工業」の定義を教えてください。
> Could you define the term "heavy industry"?

❖ 答えよう

A1 Have you ever visited a shipyard?
はい。// いいえ。// はい、あります。// いいえ、ありません。
Yes. // No. // Yes, I have. // No, I haven't.

A2 What are some parts of Japan known for manufacturing?
日本には、太平洋岸にそって、京浜、京葉、東海、中京　阪神、瀬戸内、そして　北九州の７つの主な工業地帯があります。
We have seven major manufacturing areas along the pacific coast: Keihin, Keiyo, Tokai, Chukyo, Hanshin, Setouchi, and Kitakyushu.

B1 Could you define the term "heavy industry"?
①重工業とは、飛行機や高層ビルやダムなどの大型の製品・設備、及び、鉄鋼やプラスチックなどの原材料を製造する業種のことを言います。

Heavy industry refers to the manufacture of large-scale products or equipment such as airplanes, skyscrapers, and dams, as well as materials such as steel and plastics.

②それらの製造業者は、普通、商品や生産物を、消費者ではなく、他の産業に供給します。

These manufacturers usually supply goods and products to other industries rather than to consumers.

③重工業は、国のインフラを作り、その繁栄に寄与するために必要なものです。

Heavy industry is necessary to build the infrastructure of a country and contributes to its prosperity.

④重工業は、多くの場合、多大な投資と多数の雇用によって成り立っています。

It typically relies on substantial investment and the employment of many people.

❖ 練習しよう：❶ 単語ごとに英訳しよう
　　　　　　❷「／」ごとに英訳しよう

B1 Could you define the term "heavy industry"?

①重工業　言及する　／に　その　製造　／の　大きなスケールの　製品

Heavy industry refers / to the manufacture / of large-scale products

／または　設備　／のような　飛行機　／高層ビル　／そして　ダム

/ or equipment / such as airplanes, / skyscrapers, / and dams,

／もまた　原材料　／のような　鉄鋼　そして　プラスチック。

/ as well as materials / such as steel and plastics.

②これらの　製造業者　普通　供給する　／商品　そして　生産物

These manufacturers usually supply / goods and products

／に　他の　産業　／というよりむしろ　／に　消費者。

/ to other industries / rather than / to consumers.

③重工業　だ　必要　／ために　建てる　その　インフラストラクチャー

Heavy industry is necessary / to build the infrastructure

／の　1つの　国　／そして　貢献する　／に　それの　繁栄

/ of a country / and contributes / to its prosperity.

④それ　典型的に　頼る　／に　相当な　投資　／そして　その　雇用

It typically relies / on substantial investment / and the employment

／の　たくさんの　人々。

/ of many people.

❖ 覚えよう

B1 **Could you define the term "heavy industry"?**

Heavy industry refers to the manufacture of large-scale products or equipment such as airplanes, skyscrapers, and dams, as well as materials such as steel and plastics. These manufacturers usually supply goods and products to other industries rather than to consumers. Heavy industry is necessary to build the infrastructure of a country and contributes to its prosperity. It typically relies on substantial investment and the employment of many people.

❖ 話してみよう

> **A1** Where did heavy industry develop in Japan?
>
> **A2** Why are the major heavy industrial areas located near bays in Japan?
>
> **B1** Would you describe the background of a major heavy industry and why it has been successful?

72 Light Industry
軽工業・機械工業

❖ **質問しよう**

> **A1** 今まで大工仕事をしたことがありますか。
> Have you ever done carpentry?
>
> **A2** 世界で靴と衣類の製造で有名な地域をいくつか挙げてください。
> What parts of the world are known for manufacturing shoes and clothing?
>
> **B1** 軽工業と重工業の違いを説明してください。
> Could you explain the difference between light industry and heavy industry?

❖ **答えよう**

A1 **Have you ever done carpentry?**
はい。// いいえ。// はい、あります。// いいえ、ありません。
Yes. // No. // Yes, I have. // No, I haven't.

A2 **What parts of the world are known for manufacturing shoes and clothing?**
今日、靴や衣類など私たちが購入する多くの製品は中国で製造されています。
These days, so many of the products we buy have been manufactured in China, including shoes and clothing.

B1 **Could you explain the difference between light industry and heavy industry?**
①重工業という言葉は船や橋などを含む、大きくて重い物の製造を指しています。
The term "heavy industry" refers to the manufacture of large, heavy things, including ships and bridges.

72 Light Industry 軽工業・機械工業

②一方、軽工業は、衣類や家庭電化製品など、より小さな物の製造を指します。

"Light industry," on the other hand, refers to the manufacture of smaller items, such as clothes and consumer electronics.

③重要なことは、ある国の発展の過程において、軽工業は重工業に先行するということです。

More importantly, in the process of the development of a country, light industry precedes heavy industry.

④第二次世界大戦後の日本では、重工業ができる以前には、軽工業が経済の主要な部分を担っていました。

In Japan, after the Second World War, light industry comprised the major part of the economy before heavy industry was possible.

❖ 練習しよう：❶ 単語ごとに英訳しよう
　　　　　　　❷「 / 」ごとに英訳しよう

B1 Could you explain the difference between light industry and heavy industry?

①その　用語　重工業　/言及する　に　その　製造

The term "heavy industry" / refers to the manufacture

/の　大きい　重い　もの　/含んでいる　船　そして　橋。

/ of large, heavy things, / including ships and bridges.

②軽工業　/一方　/言及する　に　その　製造

"Light industry," / on the other hand, / refers to the manufacture

/の　より小さい　品目　/のような　衣類　/そして　家庭電化製品。

/ of smaller items, / such as clothes / and consumer electronics.

③より　重要に　/に　その　プロセス　の　その　発展　/の　1つの　国

More importantly, / in the process of the development / of a country,

/軽工業　先行する　/重工業。

/ light industry precedes / heavy industry.

216

④に 日本 /後 その 第二次世界大戦
In Japan, / after the Second World War,

/軽工業 形造る /その 主要な 部分 の その 経済
/ light industry comprised / the major part of the economy

/前 /重工業 だった 可能。
/ before / heavy industry was possible.

❖ 覚えよう

B1 **Could you explain the difference between light industry and heavy industry?**

The term "heavy industry" refers to the manufacture of large, heavy things, including ships and bridges. "Light industry," on the other hand, refers to the manufacture of smaller items, such as clothes and consumer electronics. More importantly, in the process of the development of a country, light industry precedes heavy industry. In Japan, after the Second World War, light industry comprised the major part of the economy before heavy industry was possible.

❖ 話してみよう

A1 Have you ever worked in a food processing plant?

A2 Where are the major textile industrial areas in Japan?

B1 Why do you think Japan has been so successful in the consumer electronics market?

73 Construction & Engineering
建設・土木

❖ 質問しよう

A1 あなたは今までに東京タワーに上ったことがありますか。
Have you ever been to the top of Tokyo Tower?

A2 日本で最も高い建物は何ですか。またその高さを教えてください。
What is the tallest building in Japan, and how tall is it?

B1 東京スカイツリーの独特な形状を説明してください。
Could you describe the unique appearance of Tokyo Skytree?

❖ 答えよう

A1 **Have you ever been to the top of Tokyo Tower?**
はい。// いいえ。// はい、あります。// いいえ、ありません。// 2回です。// 1度もありません。
Yes. // No. // Yes, I have. // No, I haven't. // Twice. // Never.

A2 **What is the tallest building in Japan, and how tall is it?**
最も高い建物は、大阪にあるあべのハルカスだと思います。それは300メートルの高さがあります。
I think the tallest building is Abeno Harukasu in Osaka, which stands three hundred meters.

B1 **Could you describe the unique appearance of Tokyo Skytree?**

①東京スカイツリーを眺めると、それが本当に際立っていることがわかります。
When you look at Tokyo Skytree, it definitely stands out.

②634メートルの高さがあるので、他のまわりのものがとても小さく見えます。
At six hundred thirty-four meters tall, it dwarfs everything around it.

73 Construction & Engineering 建設・土木

③また、タワーの色は白ですが、夜になると色とりどりの明かりでよく照らされています。

I would say it's white in color but it's often illuminated in different colors at night.

④それは筒の形をしており、展望台が等の約4分の3の高さに位置していて、その頂上3分の1は長く、細いアンテナになっています。

It has a cylinder shape to it and an observatory is located about three-quarters of the way up the tower and the top third is a long, thin antenna.

❖ 練習しよう：❶ 単語ごとに英訳しよう
　　　　　　❷「／」ごとに英訳しよう

B1 Could you describe the unique appearance of Tokyo Skytree?

①時　あなた　見る　東京スカイツリー　／それ　断然　目立つ。
When you look at Tokyo Skytree, / it definitely stands out.

②で　634　メートル　高い　／それ　小さく見せる　すべてのもの
At six hundred thirty-four meters tall, / it dwarfs everything

／まわりの　それ。
/ around it.

③私　だろう　言う　／それだ　白い　に　色　／しかし
I would say / it's white in color / but

／それだ　しばしば　照らされる　／に　異なる　色　／に　夜。
/ it's often illuminated / in different colors / at night.

④それ　持つ　／1つの　シリンダー　形　に　それ　／そして
It has / a cylinder shape to it / and

／1つの　展望台　だ　位置される　／だいたい　4分の3　の　その　道
/ an observatory is located / about three-quarters of the way

／の上　その　タワー　／そして　その　トップ　3番め
/ up the tower / and the top third

／だ　1つの　長い　細い　アンテナ。
/ is a long, thin antenna.

❖ 覚えよう

B1 **Could you describe the unique appearance of Tokyo Skytree?**

When you look at Tokyo Skytree, it definitely stands out. At six hundred thirty-four meters tall, it dwarfs everything around it. I would say it's white in color but it's often illuminated in different colors at night. It has a cylinder shape to it and an observatory is located about three-quarters of the way up the tower and the top third is a long, thin antenna.

❖ 話してみよう

> **A1** Have you ever seen a building being constructed?
>
> **A2** What kind of training do construction workers need?
>
> **B1** What do builders in Japan do to ensure that buildings are not damaged in earthquakes?

74 Energy
エネルギー

❖ 質問しよう

> **A1** あなたの自宅にはソーラーパネルはついていますか。
> Do you have solar panels on your house?
>
> **A2** なぜ太陽光エネルギーはそれほど人気になったのでしょうか。
> Why has solar energy become so popular?
>
> **B1** 原子力のメリットとデメリットを教えてください。
> What are the advantages and disadvantages of nuclear power?

❖ 答えよう

A1 **Do you have solar panels on your house?**
はい。// いいえ。// はい、ついています。// いいえ、ついていません。// いいえ、1つも。
Yes. // No. // Yes, I do. // No, I don't. // No, none.

A2 **Why has solar energy become so popular?**
それは、クリーンで、源があふれていること、して 化石燃料への依存を減らすことができるので、人気になったと思います。
It has become popular because it is clean, the source is plentiful and it reduces our dependence on fossil fuels.

B1 **What are the advantages and disadvantages of nuclear power?**
①原子力メリットは、煙を出さないこと、天候に左右されないこと、二酸化炭素を排出しないこと、そしてそのエネルギーの密度です。
The advantages of nuclear power are that it does not produce smoke particles, does not depend on the weather, does not contribute to carbon emissions, and is the most concentrated form of energy.

②一方で、主なデメリットは核廃棄物の処理が難しいことです。
The main disadvantage is that it's difficult to dispose of nuclear waste.

③また原子力発電所の廃炉には時間とコストがかかることもあります。
Also, decommissioning nuclear power plants takes a long time and is expensive.

④最後に、たいていの方はご存じだと思いますが、原子力事故は放射能の拡散を引き起こしうること、そしてそれは人間にとても有害であることです。
Finally, as most people know, nuclear accidents can result in the spread of radiation, which is very harmful to humans.

❖ 練習しよう：❶ 単語ごとに英訳しよう
　　　　　　　❷「／」ごとに英訳しよう

B1 What are the advantages and disadvantages of nuclear power?

①その　利点　の　核の　力　／だ　ということ
The advantages of nuclear power / are that

／それ　する　ない　製造する　煙　粒子
/ it does not produce smoke particles,

／する　ない　依存する　に　その　天候
/ does not depend on the weather,

／する　ない　貢献する　に　二酸化炭素　排出
/ does not contribute to carbon emissions,

／そして　だ　その　最も　集中される　形　／の　エネルギー。
/ and is the most concentrated form / of energy.

②その　主な　不利点　だ　／ということ　それだ　難しい　捨てること
The main disadvantage is / that it's difficult to dispose

／の　核の　ごみ。
/ of nuclear waste.

③また　／廃炉すること　核の　発電所　／かかる　1つの　長い　時間
Also, / decommissioning nuclear power plants / takes a long time

/ そして　だ　高価。
/ and is expensive.

④最後に　/ように　ほとんどの　人々　知る
Finally, / as most people know,

/ 核の　事故　できる　帰結する　/ に　その　広がり　の　放射能
/ nuclear accidents can result / in the spread of radiation,

/ それ　だ　とても　有害　/ に　人間。
/ which is very harmful / to humans.

❖ 覚えよう

B1 **What are the advantages and disadvantages of nuclear power?**

The advantages of nuclear power are that it does not produce smoke particles, does not depend on the weather, does not contribute to carbon emissions, and is the most concentrated form of energy. The main disadvantage is that it's difficult to dispose of nuclear waste. Also, decommissioning nuclear power plants takes a long time and is expensive. Finally, as most people know, nuclear accidents can result in the spread of radiation, which is very harmful to humans.

❖ 話してみよう

> **A1** Have you ever seen a wind turbine in Japan?
> **A2** What are some common sources of energy?
> **B1** What are the benefits and drawbacks of wind power?

75 Agriculture & Forestry
農林業

❖ 質問しよう

A1 あなたは今まで野菜を育てたことがありますか。
Have you ever grown vegetables?

A2 特定の穀物の栽培で有名な日本の県の名前をいくつか挙げてください。
Could you name some Japanese prefectures that are famous for certain crops?

B1 自分で野菜を育てることの利点をいくつか教えてください。
What are some of the advantages of growing your own vegetables instead of purchasing them?

❖ 答えよう

A1 Have you ever grown vegetables?
はい。// いいえ。// はい、あります。// いいえ、ありません。// レタスです。
Yes. // No. // Yes, I have. // No, I haven't. // Lettuce.

A2 Could you name some Japanese prefectures that are famous for certain crops?
秋田県では多くのお米が、静岡県ではお茶が作られ、そして千葉県は落花生で有名です。
A lot of rice is grown in Akita prefecture; Shizuoka produces a lot of tea; and Chiba is famous for peanuts.

B1 What are some of the advantages of growing your own vegetables instead of purchasing them?
①もし自分で野菜を作るなら、その作物に使う化学物質の種類をコントロールできます。
If you grow your own vegetables, you have control over the kinds of chemicals that come into contact with the plants.

②スーパーで野菜を買うと、どんな農薬や肥料が使われてきたのかは決してわかりません。

When you buy vegetables at the supermarket, you can never be sure what kinds of pesticides and fertilizers have been used.

③しかしながら、自分で育てれば、これらの農薬や肥料を使うか否かは自分自身で決められます。

However, if you grow your own, it's up to you whether or not to use these products.

❖ 練習しよう：❶ 単語ごとに英訳しよう
　　　　　　 ❷「/」ごとに英訳しよう

B1 What are some of the advantages of growing your own vegetables instead of purchasing them?

①もし　あなた　育てる　/あなたの　自身の　野菜
If you grow / your own vegetables,

/あなた　持つ　コントロール　/の上に　その　種類　の　化学物質
/ you have control / over the kinds of chemicals

/それ　来る　の中に　接触　/と一緒に　その　植物。
/ that come into contact / with the plants.

②時　あなた　買う　野菜　/で　その　スーパー
When you buy vegetables / at the supermarket,

/あなた　できる　決してない　だ　確信的　/何　種類　の　農薬
/ you can never be sure / what kinds of pesticides

/そして　肥料　/持つ　だった　使われる。
/ and fertilizers / have been used.

③しかしながら　/もし　あなた　育てる　あなたの　自身の
However, / if you grow your own,

/それだ　〜次第　あなた　/かどうか　または　ない
/ it's up to you / whether or not

/使うこと　これらの　製品。
/ to use these products.

❖ 覚えよう

B1 **What are some of the advantages of growing your own vegetables instead of purchasing them?**

If you grow your own vegetables, you have control over the kinds of chemicals that come into contact with the plants. When you buy vegetables at the supermarket, you can never be sure what kinds of pesticides and fertilizers have been used. However, if you grow your own, it's up to you whether or not to use these products.

❖ 話してみよう

> **A1** When you buy vegetables, do you check where they were grown?
>
> **A2** What are some of the challenges Japanese farmers face?
>
> **B1** Could you describe the role of forestry in today's world?

76 The Fishing Industry
水産業

❖ 質問しよう

A1 あなたはマグロの刺身が好きですか。
Do you like tuna *sashimi*?

A2 世界のどこで通常マグロは捕獲されていますか。
What part of the world are tuna usually caught in?

B1 漁師がどのようにマグロを獲るか教えてください。
Could you explain how fishermen catch tuna?

❖ 答えよう

A1 Do you like tuna *sashimi*?
はい。// いいえ。// はい、好きです。// 大好きです。// あまり。
Yes. // No. // Yes, I do. // Very much. // Not so much.

A2 What part of the world are tuna usually caught in?
ほとんどのマグロが太平洋上で捕獲されています。
Most tuna are caught in the Pacific Ocean.

B1 Could you explain how fishermen catch tuna?
①漁師は2、3の異なる方法でマグロを捕獲します。
Fishermen catch tuna in a few different ways.

②最も一般的な方法は、まき網漁と呼ばれています。
The most popular way is through a method called purse seining.

③この方法では、漁師は大きく、上に網を支える浮きがつき円を描くように作られた網を使い、それを沈めてその中に魚を捕獲します。
With this method, fishermen use a large, circular net with floats holding the net on top and then squeeze the bottom thereby trapping the fish in it.

76 The Fishing Industry 水産業

④もう1つの方法は、延縄漁と呼ばれ、1本の長い釣り糸から餌のついた針を垂らして行う方法です。

Another method is called longlining, which is a long line with baited hooks hanging from it.

⑤1本釣りと呼ばれる伝統的な方法では、マグロを1匹ずつ釣り上げます。

There is a traditional method called pole and line fishing by which the tuna are caught one by one.

❖ 練習しよう：❶ 単語ごとに英訳しよう
❷「/」ごとに英訳しよう

B1 Could you explain how fishermen catch tuna?

①漁師　捕まえる　マグロ　/に　2、3の　異なる　方法。
Fishermen catch tuna / in a few different ways.

②その　最も　一般的な　方法　だ　/通して　1つ　方法
The most popular way is / through a method

/ 呼ばれる　まき網漁。
/ called purse seining.

③で　この　方法　/漁師　使う　1つの　大きい　丸い　網
With this method, / fishermen use a large, circular net

/と一緒に　浮き　/つかんでいる　その　網　に　上
/ with floats / holding the net on top

/そして　それから　絞る　その　底　/それによって
/ and then squeeze the bottom / thereby

/捕える　その　魚　に　それ。
/ trapping the fish in it.

④もう1つの　方法　だ　/呼ばれる　延縄
Another method is / called longlining,

/それは　だ　1つの　長い　釣り糸　/と一緒に　餌が付いている　針
/ which is a long line / with baited hooks

/垂れている から それ。
/ hanging from it.

⑤ある 1つの 伝統的な 方法 /呼ばれる 1本釣り
There is a traditional method / called pole and line fishing

/によって それ /その マグロ だ 捕まえられる /1つひとつ。
/ by which / the tuna are caught / one by one.

❖ 覚えよう

B1 Could you explain how fishermen catch tuna?

Fishermen catch tuna in a few different ways. The most popular way is through a method called purse seining. With this method, fishermen use a large, circular net with floats holding the net on top and then squeeze the bottom thereby trapping the fish in it. Another method is called longlining, which is a long line with baited hooks hanging from it. There is a traditional method called pole and line fishing by which the tuna are caught one by one.

❖ 話してみよう

A1 Do you like to go fishing?

A2 Could you talk about the importance of the fishing industry to Japan?

B1 How have human factors, such as pollution, affected the fishing industry?

77 Accidents
事件・事故

❖ 質問しよう

> **A1** 交通事故を見たことがありますか。
> Have you seen a traffic accident?
>
> **A2** 交通事故の一般的な原因をいくつか挙げてください。
> What are some common causes of traffic accidents?
>
> **B1** 交通事故を減らすために、科学技術をどのように使うことができますか。
> How can technology be used to reduce traffic accidents?

❖ 答えよう

A1 **Have you seen a traffic accident?**
はい。// いいえ。// はい、あります。// いいえ、ありません。// いいえ、一度も。
Yes. // No. // Yes, I have. // No, I haven't. // No, never.

A2 **What are some common causes of traffic accidents?**
車を運転する際に携帯電話を使ったり、お酒を飲んでいたりすると、事故を起こしやすいです。
When people are using their phones while driving or when they drink alcohol, they are more likely to have an accident.

B1 **How can technology be used to reduce traffic accidents?**
①交通事故を減らすための、さらに多くの科学技術の進歩を、私たちは目の当たりにするだろうと思います。

I think we will see more and more technological advances that reduce traffic accidents.

②自動車会社は、多くの事故を防ぐ自動ブレーキシステムをすでに開発しています。

Automobile companies have already developed automatic

braking systems that prevent many accidents.

③そしてまもなく、私たちは、自動運転車を路上で見かけることになるでしょう。
And soon we will see self-driving cars on the road.

④もしこの科学技術が効果的に実現すれば、交通事故がはるかに少なくなるでしょう。
If this technology is implemented effectively, we should see far fewer traffic accidents.

❖ 練習しよう：❶ 単語ごとに英訳しよう
❷「 / 」ごとに英訳しよう

B1 How can technology be used to reduce traffic accidents?

①私 思う ／私たち 見る ／より そして より 科学技術の 進歩
I think / we will see / more and more technological advances

／それ 引き下げる 交通 事故。
/ that reduce traffic accidents.

②自動車 会社 ／持つ すでに 開発した
Automobile companies / have already developed

／自動の ブレーキング システム ／それ 防ぐ 多くの 事故。
/ automatic braking systems / that prevent many accidents.

③そして ／まもなく ／私たち だろう 見る ／自動運転車
And / soon / we will see / self-driving cars

／の上で その 道路。
/ on the road.

④もし ／この 科学技術 だ 実行される ／効果的に
If / this technology is implemented / effectively,

／私たち べき 見る ／はるかに より少ない 交通 事故。
/ we should see / far fewer traffic accidents.

❖ 覚えよう

B1 **How can technology be used to reduce traffic accidents?**

I think we will see more and more technological advances that reduce traffic accidents. Automobile companies have already developed automatic braking systems that prevent many accidents. And soon we will see self-driving cars on the road. If this technology is implemented effectively, we should see far fewer traffic accidents.

❖ 話してみよう

> **A1** Have you ever had a bicycle accident?
>
> **A2** What is one thing everyone can do to avoid accidents at home?
>
> **B1** Can you describe a situation in which an accident could lead to a positive outcome?

78 Discrimination
差別

❖ **質問しよう**

> **A1** あなたは今までに差別されたと感じたことがありますか。
> Have you ever felt that you were discriminated against?
>
> **A2** あなたが知っている差別の例を教えてください。
> Can you share an example of discrimination that you know about?
>
> **B1** あなたの意見では、差別に対応する最善の方法は何ですか。
> In your opinion, what is the best way to respond to discrimination?

❖ **答えよう**

A1 **Have you ever felt that you were discriminated against?**
はい。// いいえ。// はい、あります。// いいえ、ありません。// いいえ、あまり。
Yes. // No. // Yes, I have. // No, I haven't. // No, not really.

A2 **Can you share an example of discrimination that you know about?**
私の友人の父親が解雇され、そして彼はその理由は彼の年齢のせいだと思っています。これは、年齢差別の例かもしれません。
My friend's father was fired from his job, and he thinks it was because of his age. This might be an example of age discrimination.

B1 **In your opinion, what is the best way to respond to discrimination?**
①人や状況によりますが、私は、差別に対応する際に最も重要なポイントの1つは、自分自身を大切にすることだと思います。
It depends on the individual and the situation, but I think one

of the most important points when dealing with discrimination is taking care of yourself.

②信頼できる友人や家族と話し、何が起きているのかを知ってもらうことも重要です。
It's also important to talk with trusted friends or family members to let them know what's going on.

③話を聞いてくれる人がいるだけで、ストレスが和らぐことがあります。
Sometimes just talking with a good listener can relieve stress.

④気持ちが落ち着いてから、正式な抗議を行うなど、次に何をするか決めればいいです。
After you feel calm, you can decide what to do next, such as making a formal complaint.

❖ 練習しよう：❶ 単語ごとに英訳しよう
　　　　　　❷「/」ごとに英訳しよう

B1 In your opinion, what is the best way to respond to discrimination?

①それ 依る /に その 個人 /そして その 状況
It depends / on the individual / and the situation,

/しかし /私 思う /1つ の その 最も 重要な ポイント
/ but / I think / one of the most important points

/時 扱う と一緒に 差別 /だ 面倒をみること の あなた自身。
/ when dealing with discrimination / is taking care of yourself.

②それだ また 重要 /話すこと と一緒に 信頼される 友達
It's also important / to talk with trusted friends

/または 家族 メンバー /ため 許す 彼ら 知る
/ or family members / to let them know

/何だ 起こっている。
/ what's going on.

③時々 /ちょうど 話すこと と一緒に 1つの よい 聞き手
Sometimes / just talking with a good listener

/ できる 和らげる ストレス。
/ can relieve stress.

④後 あなた 感じる 穏やか / あなた できる 決める
After you feel calm, / you can decide

/ 何 すること 次に / のような / 作ること 正式な 不平。
/ what to do next, / such as / making a formal complaint.

❖ 覚えよう

B1 **In your opinion, what is the best way to respond to discrimination?**

It depends on the individual and the situation, but I think one of the most important points when dealing with discrimination is taking care of yourself. It's also important to talk with trusted friends or family members to let them know what's going on. Sometimes just talking with a good listener can relieve stress. After you feel calm, you can decide what to do next, such as making a formal complaint.

❖ 話してみよう

A1 Do you think discrimination exists in all countries?

A2 Could you give a basic definition of the word discrimination?

B1 What is the main cause of discrimination?

79 Aging Society & Falling Birthrate
少子高齢化

❖ 質問しよう

> **A1** あなたは日本の高齢化社会と出生率の低下の問題について聞いたことがありますか。
> Have you heard about the issue in Japan of the aging society and falling birthrate?
>
> **A2** あなたは高齢者の生活はどのようなものだと思いますか。
> What do you think life as an elderly person will be like for you?
>
> **B1** 少子高齢化の不都合な点を1つ説明してください。
> Could you explain one of the disadvantages of the aging society and falling birthrate?

❖ 答えよう

A1 **Have you heard about the issue in Japan of the aging society and falling birthrate?**

はい。// いいえ。// はい、あります。// いいえ、ありません。// もちろんです。

Yes. // No. // Yes, I have. // No, I haven't. // Of course.

A2 **What do you think life as an elderly person will be like for you?**

私は買い物や、電車に乗ること、また歩くといった日常的なことが少し難しくなるだろうと思います。

I think it will be a bit difficult to do everyday things like shopping, riding the train and walking.

79 Aging Society & Falling Birthrate 少子高齢化

B1 **Could you explain one of the disadvantages of the aging society and falling birthrate?**

①1つの問題は、それが社会保障制度に悪い影響を与えることです。

One problem is that it negatively impacts the social security system.

②少子高齢化が進んだ国では、労働者より退職者の方が相対的に多く、また、労働者は退職者を支えることが期待されるので、労働者には大きな負担がかかります。

In a country with an aging society and falling birth rate, there are relatively more retired than employed people, and this puts a greater burden on those in the workforce because they are expected to support the retired.

③つまり、社会保障制度を維持するために、若い人たちがより多く払わなければならないということです。

In other words, younger people have to pay much more to maintain the social security system.

❖ 練習しよう：❶ 単語ごとに英訳しよう
　　　　　　　❷「／」ごとに英訳しよう

B1 **Could you explain one of the disadvantages of the aging society and falling birthrate?**

①1つの　問題　だ　ということ　／それ　否定的に　インパクトを与える

One problem is that / it negatively impacts

／その　社会保障制度。

/ the social security system.

②に　1つの　国　／と一緒に　1つの　少子高齢化

In a country / with an aging society and falling birth rate,

／そこに　ある　相対的に　／より多くの　退職者

/ there are relatively / more retired

／よりも　雇用される　人々　／そして　これ　置く

/ than employed people, / and this puts

/1つの より大きな 負荷 /の上に それら /に その 労働人口
/ a greater burden / on those / in the workforce

/なぜなら /彼ら だ 期待される /支えること その 退職者。
/ because / they are expected / to support the retired.

③言い換えれば /より若い 人々 なければならない 払う
In other words, / younger people have to pay

/ずっと より多く /ために 維持する その 社会保障制度。
/ much more / to maintain the social security system.

❖ 覚えよう

B1 **Could you explain one of the disadvantages of the aging society and falling birthrate?**

One problem is that it negatively impacts the social security system. In a country with an aging society and falling birth rate, there are relatively more retired than employed people, and this puts a greater burden on those in the workforce because they are expected to support the retired. In other words, younger people have to pay much more to maintain the social security system.

❖ 話してみよう

A1 Is the aging society and falling birthrate situation getting better?

A2 When was the last time you heard about problems related to the aging society and falling birthrate?

B1 Could you propose a solution to the aging society and falling birthrate problem?

80 Social Security & Welfare
社会保障・福祉

❖ 質問しよう

> **A1** あなたは健康保険に加入していますか。
> Are you a member of a health insurance program?
>
> **A2** あなたはどのくらいの頻度で健康保険を使いますか。
> How often do you use your health insurance?
>
> **B1** 日本の社会保障制度の1つの側面を説明してください。
> Could you explain one aspect of the Japanese social security system?

❖ 答えよう

A1 **Are you a member of a health insurance program?**
はい。// いいえ。// はい、加入しています。// いいえ、加入していません。
Yes. // No/ // Yes, I am. // No, I'm not.

A2 **How often do you use your health insurance?**
私はだいたい年に3、4回健康保険を使います。風邪をひいたり、インフルエンザにかかったり、そして、薬が必要な時に使います。
I use my health insurance about three or four times a year. I use it when I have a bad cold or the flu and need medicine.

B1 **Could you explain one aspect of the Japanese social security system?**
①日本に住む人全員がこの制度に加入しており、つまり、みなでそれを負担して、みなが保障されます。

Everyone living in Japan takes part in this system, which means that they all pay to support it and are covered by it.

②健康保険は、このシステムの1つの側面です。

Health insurance is one aspect of the system.

③基本的に患者にかかった医療費の70%はこの制度で保証され、被保険者は残りの30%を負担します。

Basically seventy percent of the medical expenses incurred by patients are covered under the present system while the insured must pay for the remaining thirty percent.

④この支払方法は歯科にも適用されます。

This payment plan also applies to dental expenses.

❖ 練習しよう：❶ 単語ごとに英訳しよう
　　　　　　❷「／」ごとに英訳しよう

B1 Could you explain one aspect of the Japanese social security system?

①すべての人　住んでいる　に　日本　／参加する　この　システム

Everyone living in Japan / takes part in this system,

／それ　意味する　／ということ　彼ら　すべて　払う

/ which means / that they all pay

／ため　支える　それ　／そして　だ　カバーされる　によって　それ。

/ to support it / and are covered by it.

②健康保険　／だ　1つの　側面　／の　その　システム。

Health insurance / is one aspect / of the system.

③基本的に　／70%　の　その　医療の　費用

Basically / seventy percent of the medical expenses

／負担される　によって　患者

/ incurred by patients

／だ　カバーされる　の下に　その　現在の　システム

/ are covered under the present system

／一方　／その　被保険者　しなければならない　払う

/ while / the insured must pay

／のため　その　残っている　30%。

/ for the remaining thirty percent.

④この 支払い 計画 / また 適用する / に 歯科の 費用。
This payment plan / also applies / to dental expenses.

❖ 覚えよう

B1 **Could you explain one aspect of the Japanese social security system?**

Everyone living in Japan takes part in this system, which means that they all pay to support it and are covered by it. Health insurance is one aspect of the system. Basically seventy percent of the medical expenses incurred by patients are covered under the present system while the insured must pay for the remaining thirty percent. This payment plan also applies to dental expenses.

❖ 話してみよう

A1 Do you think Japan can support the current social security system in the future?

A2 What kind of support do Japanese people get from our social security system?

B1 Can you suggest a solution to solve the current issues relating to our social security system?

81 Politics
政治

❖ 質問しよう

A1 あなたは政治に興味がありますか。
Are you interested in politics?

A2 なぜあなたは政治に興味がある／ないのですか。
Why are/aren't you interested in politics?

B1 日本の国会について説明してください。
Could you explain the Japanese Diet?

❖ 答えよう

A1 Are you interested in politics?
はい。// いいえ。// はい、興味があります。// いいえ、興味がありません。// 少し。// まったく。
Yes. // No. // Yes, I am. // No, I'm not. // A little. // Not at all.

A2 Why are/aren't you interested in politics?
私はただその問題にあまりついていけません。政治家の説明は私にはあまりにわかりにくいです。
I just can't follow the issues very well. The politicians' explanations are too complicated for me.

B1 Could you explain the Japanese Diet?

①日本の国会は二院制で、衆議院と参議院に分かれています。
The Japanese Diet is divided into two houses: the House of Representatives and the House of Councilors.

②国会は法を整備し国権の最高組織です。
The Diet makes laws and is the highest organ of state power.

③衆議院の定員は475で、在任期間は4年です。
There are 475 members in the House of Representatives, whose term of office is four years.

④参議院の定員は242で、在任期間は6年です。
There are 242 members in the House of Councilors, and their term of office is six years.

⑤両院ともたいていの場合ほぼ同じ力を持ちますが、衆議院の決定は、参議院のそれよりも優先されます。
Both Houses have the same power in most cases, but the decisions of the House of Representatives precede those of the House of Councilors.

❖ 練習しよう：❶ 単語ごとに英訳しよう
　　　　　　❷「／」ごとに英訳しよう

B1 Could you explain the Japanese Diet?

①その　日本の　国会　だ　／分けられる　の中に　２つの　院
The Japanese Diet is / divided into two houses:

／その　衆議院　／そして　その　参議院。
/ the House of Representatives / and the House of Councilors.

②その　国会　作る　法律　／そして　だ　その　最も高い　機関
The Diet makes laws / and is the highest organ

／の　国　パワー。
/ of state power.

③そこに　ある　475　メンバー　／に　その　衆議院
There are 475 members / in the House of Representatives,

／それの　期間　の　職務　／だ　4　年。
/ whose term of office / is four years.

④そこに　ある　242　メンバー　／に　その　参議院
There are 242 members / in the House of Councilors,

／そして　彼らの　期間　の　職務　／だ　6　年。
/ and their term of office / is six years.

⑤両方の　院　持つ　その　同じ　パワー　／に　ほとんどの　ケース
Both Houses have the same power / in most cases,

/ しかし　その　決定　の　その　衆議院
/ but the decisions of the House of Representatives

/ 優先する　それら　の　その　参議院。
/ precede those of the House of Councilors.

❖ 覚えよう

B1 **Could you explain the Japanese Diet?**

The Japanese Diet is divided into two houses: the House of Representatives and the House of Councilors. The Diet makes laws and is the highest organ of state power. There are 475 members in the House of Representatives, whose term of office is four years. There are 242 members in the House of Councilors, and their term of office is six years. Both Houses have the same power in most cases, but the decisions of the House of Representatives precede those of the House of Councilors.

❖ 話してみよう

> **A1** Who is the current prime minister of Japan?
> **A2** Why do you think people become politicians?
> **B1** Which political party do you most agree with and why?

82 Law
法律

❖ 質問しよう

A1 あなたは日本国憲法第9条について詳しく知っていますか。
Do you know much about Article 9 in the Japanese Constitution?

A2 あなたは日本国憲法第9条についていつどこで学びましたか。
When and where did you learn about Article 9 of the Japanese Constitution?

B1 日本国憲法第9条のよい点と悪い点を説明してください。
Could you explain a good point and a bad point of Article 9?

❖ 答えよう

A1 Do you know much about Article 9 in the Japanese Constitution?

はい。// いいえ。// はい、知っています。// いいえ、知りません。
Yes. // No. // Yes, I do. // No, I don't.

A2 When and where did you learn about Article 9 of the Japanese Constitution?

私は中高の社会科の授業で第9条について学びました。
I learned about Article 9 in my middle school social studies class.

B1 Could you explain a good point and a bad point of Article 9?

①えー、第9条のよい点は日本政府が国際紛争を解決する手段として軍事力を使うことを禁止している点だと言う人がいます。
Well, some people say that the good point about Article 9 is that it prohibits the Japanese government from using its military forces as a means of resolving international disputes.

②これは、日本が戦争を始められないということを意味しています。
This means Japan cannot start a war.

③悪い点は他国からの攻撃に対応する日本の能力を第9条が制限している点だと言う人もいます。
Others say the bad point is that Article 9 limits Japan's ability to respond to an attack from another country.

④つまり、このようなことが起こった場合には、日本は他の国からの軍事支援を要請せざるを得ないということです。
If this happened, in other words, Japan would have to request military assistance from other nations.

❖ 練習しよう：❶ 単語ごとに英訳しよう
　　　　　　　❷「 / 」ごとに英訳しよう

B1 Could you explain a good point and a bad point of Article 9?

①えー / 何人かの　人々　言う
Well, / some people say

/ ということ　/ その　よい　点　について　9条
/ that / the good point about Article 9

/ だ　ということ　/ それ　禁止する　その　日本の　政府
/ is that / it prohibits the Japanese government

/ から　使うこと　それの　軍の　力
/ from using its military forces

/ として　1つの　手段 / の　解決すること　国際的な　紛争。
/ as a means / of resolving international disputes.

②これ　意味する　/ 日本　できない　スタートする / 1つの　戦争。
This means / Japan cannot start / a war.

③他の人たち　言う　/ その　悪い　点　だ / ということ
Others say / the bad point is / that

/ 第9条　制限する　/ 日本の　能力　/ 対応するため
/ Article 9 limits / Japan's ability / to respond

/に 1つの 攻撃 /から 他の 国。
/ to an attack / from another country.

④もし これ 起こった /言い換えれば
If this happened, / in other words,

/日本 だろう なければならない 要求する /軍事の 支援
/ Japan would have to request / military assistance

/から 他の 国。
/ from other nations.

❖ 覚えよう

B1 **Could you explain a good point and a bad point of Article 9?**

Well, some people say that the good point about Article 9 is that it prohibits the Japanese government from using its military force as a means of resolving international disputes. This means Japan cannot start a war. Others say the bad point is that Article 9 limits Japan's ability to respond to an attack from another country. If this happened, in other words, Japan would have to request military assistance from other nations.

❖ 話してみよう

> **A1** Would you like to become a lawyer?
> **A2** How does a person become a lawyer in Japan?
> **B1** How are new laws created in Japan?

83 Social Movements
社会運動

❖ 質問しよう

A1 あなたはメーデーを知っていますか。
Do you know about May Day?

A2 日本で初めてメーデーが行われたのはいつですか。
When was May Day first observed in Japan?

B1 メーデーについて説明してください。
Could you explain May Day?

❖ 答えよう

A1 Do you know about May Day?
はい。// いいえ。// はい、知っています。// はい、少し。
Yes. // No. // Yes, I do. // Yes, a little.

A2 When was May Day first observed in Japan?
それは、1920年5月2日上野公園で開催されました。
It was held at Ueno Park on May 2nd in 1920.

B1 Could you explain May Day?

①実際には　メーデーのお祝いは紀元前のヨーロッパで夏の訪れを祝うために始まりました。

Actually, the celebration of May Day started in pre-Christian times in Europe to celebrate the coming of summer.

②ヨーロッパがキリスト教化した時、異教徒の遺産は失われましたが、人々は5月柱を立て、宴会やダンスをして、それを祝い続けました。

When Europe became Christianized, it lost its pagan heritage, but people continued to celebrate it by erecting May poles, having feasts and dancing.

③メーデーは、悲劇に終わったシカゴの労働デモを記念する政治的な行事にもなりました。
May Day also became a political celebration to commemorate a labor demonstration in Chicago, which resulted in tragedy.

④そして、メーデーは、労働者の状況に注目を集める手段として、世界中の労働者階級、特に社会主義者や共産主義者によって選択されました。
May Day was then chosen by working class people around the world, specially socialists and communists, as a way to draw attention to the conditions of laborers everywhere.

❖ 練習しよう：❶ 単語ごとに英訳しよう
　　　　　　❷「 / 」ごとに英訳しよう

B1 Could you explain May Day?

①実際 / その 祝い の メーデー
Actually, / the celebration of May Day

/ スタートした に 前キリスト教 時期
/ started in pre-Christian times

/ に ヨーロッパ / ため 祝う その 来ること の 夏。
/ in Europe / to celebrate the coming of summer.

②時 ヨーロッパ なった キリスト教化される / それ 失った
When Europe became Christianized, / it lost

/ それの 異教徒の 遺産 / しかし / 人々は 続けた 祝うこと それ
/ its pagan heritage, / but / people continued to celebrate it

/ までに 立てること 五月柱 / 持つこと 宴会 そして 踊ること。
/ by erecting May poles, / having feasts and dancing.

③メーデー / また なった 1つの 政治的な 祝い / ため 記念する
May Day / also became a political celebration / to commemorate

/ 1つの 労働 デモ / に シカゴ / それ 帰結した に 悲劇。
/ a labor demonstration / in Chicago, / which resulted in tragedy.

④メーデー だった それから 選ばれる
May Day was then chosen

/によって　ワーキングクラス　人々　/のまわり　その　世界
/ by working class people / around the world,

/特に　社会主義者　と　共産主義者　/として　1つの　方法
/ especially socialists and communists, / as a way

ため　引く　注意　/に　その　状況　の　労働者　どこでも。
/ to draw attention / to the conditions of laborers everywhere.

❖ 覚えよう

B1 Could you explain May Day?

Actually, the celebration of May Day started in pre-Christian times in Europe to celebrate the coming of summer. When Europe became Christianized, it lost its pagan heritage, but people continued to celebrate it by erecting May poles, having feasts and dancing. May Day also became a political celebration to commemorate a labor demonstration in Chicago, which resulted in tragedy. May Day was then chosen by working class people around the world, especially socialists and communists, as a way to draw attention to the conditions of laborers everywhere.

❖ 話してみよう

> **A1** Do you know of any social movements in Japan?
> **A2** What kinds of social movements were initiated after the Tohoku Earthquake of 2011?
> **B1** What kinds of social movements have the greatest chance of creating major changes?

84 Elections
選挙

❖ 質問しよう

A1 あなたは普段選挙に行きますか。
Do you usually vote in elections?

A2 選挙に行かない友達にアドバイスをしてください。
What would you say to a friend who does not vote?

B1 選挙が確実に公平に行われるようにするためにはどうすべきだと思いますか。
What can be done to ensure that elections are fair?

❖ 答えよう

A1 Do you usually vote in elections?
はい。// いいえ。// はい、行きます。// いいえ、行きません。// 毎回。// 1度も。

Yes. // No. // Yes, I do. // No, I don't. // Every time. // Never.

A2 What would you say to a friend who does not vote?
私は1票が大切だということを友達に伝えます。また投票することは市民としての義務だとも伝えます。

I would say to my friend that every vote counts. Also, I'd say it is your responsibility as a citizen to vote.

B1 What can be done to ensure that elections are fair?
①私達がすべきことは、偏見がなく、独立した選挙委員会に実際の選挙運営を監督させることです。

What needs to be done is to let impartial, independent, electoral commissions oversee the actual administration of elections.

②投票のルールが守られることを保証することに付け加えて、選挙運動資金に制限をかけることとメディアの利用に関するルールを設定すべきです。

Besides ensuring that the rules of voting are followed, there should also be a limit on the spending of campaign money and rules for media access.

③政治団体や個人に、政治の代表を選ぶ選挙に不公平な影響を及ぼす財政的な利点を使わせては決していけません。

No one party or individual should be allowed to use financial advantages to unfairly influence the election of political representatives.

❖ 練習しよう：❶ 単語ごとに英訳しよう
　　　　　　❷「／」ごとに英訳しよう

B1 What can be done to ensure that elections are fair?

①何　必要だ　であること　される　だ　／させること　偏らない
What needs to be done is / to let impartial,

／独立した　／選挙の　委員会
/ independent, / electoral commissions

／監督する　その　実際の　管理　／の　選挙。
/ oversee the actual administration / of elections.

②の他に　確かにする　／ということ　その　ルール　の　投票
Besides ensuring / that the rules of voting

／だ　守られる　／そこに　べき　また　だ　／1つの　制限
/ are followed, / there should also be / a limit

／に　その　消費　／の　キャンペーンの　お金
/ on the spending / of campaign money

／そして　ルール　のための　メディア　アクセス。
/ and rules for media access.

③ない　1つの　団体　または　個人　／べき　だ　許される
No one party or individual / should be allowed

/使うこと　財政的　有利さ　/ため　不公平に　影響する
/ to use financial advantages / to unfairly influence

/その　選挙　の　政治の　代表たち。
/ the election of political representatives.

❖ 覚えよう

B1 **What can be done to ensure that elections are fair?**

What needs to be done is to let impartial, independent, electoral commissions oversee the actual administration of elections. Besides ensuring that the rules of voting are followed, there should also be a limit on the spending of campaign money and rules for media access. No one party or individual should be allowed to use financial advantages to unfairly influence the election of political representatives.

❖ 話してみよう

A1 Do you think having an election is the best way to choose the leader of a country?

A2 What are some problems that might occur when elections are held?

B1 Could you explain how the prime minister of Japan is chosen?

85 Diplomacy
外交

❖ 質問しよう

A1 あなたは大使になりたいと思いますか。
Would you like to become an ambassador?

A2 大使になるよい点、あるいは悪い点を教えてください。
What are the good or bad points of becoming an ambassador?

B1 大使がどのような仕事をしているか説明してください。
Could you explain what an ambassador does?

❖ 答えよう

A1 Would you like to become an ambassador?
はい。// いいえ。// はい、なりたいです。// いいえ、なりたくないです。// たぶん。
Yes. // No. // Yes, I would. // No, I wouldn't. // Maybe.

A2 What are the good or bad points of becoming an ambassador?
それはとても面白く、派手な生活かもしれないけれど、長い間母国と離れて住むことは大変だと思います。

It seems like an exciting and even glamorous lifestyle, but it might be hard to live away from your home country for a long time.

B1 Could you explain what an ambassador does?
①大使というのは、国を代表する外交官の長です。

An ambassador is the chief diplomat who represents his or her country.

②大使は普段他国に長い間住むことになります。

He or she usually resides in another country.

85 Diplomacy 外交

③それゆえロシア駐在アメリカ大使という職名を耳にします。
　Hence, we hear titles like "The United States Ambassador to Russia."
④大使は国際的な行事に出席し、そこで自国の利益のために尽くします。
　An ambassador attends international events where he or she serves the interests of his or her country.
⑤政府の役人たちとのミーティングも大使にとって必須の仕事です。
　Meeting with government officials is an essential job for an ambassador as well.

❖ 練習しよう：❶ 単語ごとに英訳しよう
　　　　　　 ❷ 「／」ごとに英訳しよう

B1 Could you explain what an ambassador does?

① 1つの　大使　だ　／その　チーフ　外交官　／彼　代表する
　An ambassador is ／ the chief diplomat ／ who represents
　／彼の　または　彼女の　国。
　／ his or her country.
②彼　または　彼女　普段　居住する　／に　その他の　国。
　He or she usually resides ／ in another country.
③それゆえ　／私たち　聞く　肩書き　／ような
　Hence, ／ we hear titles ／ like
　／その　合衆国　大使　／に　ロシア。
　／ "The United States Ambassador ／ to Russia."
④ 1人の　大使　出席する　／国際的な　行事
　An ambassador attends ／ international events
　／そこで　彼　または　彼女　のために尽くす　／その　利益
　／ where he or she serves ／ the interests
　／の　彼の　または　彼女の　国。
　／ of his or her country.
⑤ミーティング　と一緒に　政府　役人たち　／だ　1つの　必須の　仕事
　Meeting with government officials ／ is an essential job

/ にとって 1つの 大使 / もまた。
/ for an ambassador / as well.

❖ 覚えよう

B1 **Could you explain what an ambassador does?**

An ambassador is the chief diplomat who represents his or her country. He or she usually resides in another country. Hence, we hear titles like "The United States Ambassador to Russia." An ambassador attends international events where he or she serves the interests of his or her country. Meeting with government officials is an essential job for an ambassador as well.

❖ 話してみよう

A1 Have you ever seen the Japanese prime minister talking with leaders of other countries?

A2 What do you think about Japan's relationship with other countries?

B1 Could you describe something Japan could do to improve its relationship with another country?

86 War
戦争

❖ 質問しよう

A1 あなたは今日の新聞で戦争に関する記事を読みましたか。
Did you read an article about war in today's newspaper?

A2 日本が最後に戦争に参加したのはいつですか。
When did Japan last take part in a war?

B1 戦争を起こさないために我々は何をすべきですか。
What can we do to avoid war?

❖ 答えよう

A1 Did you read an article about war in today's newspaper?
はい。// いいえ。// はい、読みました。// いいえ、読みませんでした。
Yes. // No. // Yes, I did. // No, I didn't.

A2 When did Japan last take part in a war?
日本が最後に戦争に参加したのは第二次世界大戦です。
The last war that Japan took part in was World War II.

B1 What can we do to avoid war?
①戦争は2国以上の国々の間でお互いの理解が決裂した時に起きます。

War results because of a breakdown in understanding between two or more countries.

②そのような状況を避けるためには、政治家、メディアあるいはその国の市民が、国家レベルだけでなく草の根レベルでお互いのコミュニケーションを推進することが必要です。

In order to avoid such a situation, the political representatives, the media and the citizens of each country should promote mutual communication not only at the national level but at the grassroots level as well.

③私たちが国家の問題についてオープンに話す時、顔を突き合わせることによって、怒りをかきたてるような問題の解決に向けてスタートを切ることができます。

When we talk about national problems openly, we can start to resolve inflammatory issues by putting a human face on them.

❖ 練習しよう：❶ 単語ごとに英訳しよう
❷「/」ごとに英訳しよう

B1 What can we do to avoid war?

①戦争　起こる　/せいで　1つの　決裂　に　理解
War results / because of a breakdown in understanding

/の間　2つ　または　より多い　国々。
/ between two or more countries.

②ために　避ける　/そんな　1つの　状況　/その　政治的な　代表たち
In order to avoid / such a situation, / the political representatives,

/その　メディア　/そして　その　市民　の　それぞれの　国
/ the media / and the citizens of each country

/べき　促進する　お互いの　コミュニケーション
/ should promote mutual communication

/ない　だけ　で　その　国の　レベル
/ not only at the national level

/しかし　で　その　草の根　レベル　/同様に。
/ but at the grassroots level / as well.

③時　私たち　話す　/について　国家の　問題　/オープンに
When we talk / about national problems / openly,

/私たち　できる　スタートする
/ we can start

/解決すること　怒りをかきたてる　問題
/ to resolve inflammatory issues

/によって　置くこと　1つの　人間　顔　/に　それら。
/ by putting a human face / on them.

❖ 覚えよう

B1 **What can we do to avoid war?**

War results because of a breakdown in understanding between two or more countries. In order to avoid such a situation, the political representatives, the media and the citizens of each country should promote mutual communication not only at the national level but at the grassroots level as well. When we talk about national problems openly, we can start to resolve inflammatory issues by putting a human face on them.

❖ 話してみよう

> **A1** How do you say the word "war" in Japanese?
> **A2** What are some of the causes of war?
> **B1** Could you describe a situation in which going to war would be the best choice for a country?

87 Conferences & Meetings
会議

❖ 質問しよう

A1 あなたは今までに会議に出席したことがありますか。
Have you ever attended a meeting?

A2 大学生はどんな会議に出席しますか。
What kinds of meetings do university students attend?

B1 会議の責任者はどのような点に配慮するべきかを述べてください。
Could you tell me what kind of things the person in charge of a meeting should be careful about?

❖ 答えよう

A1 **Have you ever attended a meeting?**
はい。// いいえ。// はい、あります。// いいえ、ありません。// 何度も。
Yes. // No. // Yes, I have. // No, I haven't. // Lots of them.

A2 **What kinds of meetings do university students attend?**
一般的に学生はクラブのミーティングに参加します。
It's common for students to go to club meetings.

B1 **Could you tell me what kind of things the person in charge of a meeting should be careful about?**

①リーダー、つまり会議の責任者は、会議の目的をわかりやすく説明し、メンバーが集中していることを確かめる必要があると思います。

I think the leader, the person in charge of a meeting, should clearly explain the purpose of the meeting and make sure the group stays focused.

②リーダーが全員に話すチャンスを与えることも重要だと思います。

I also think it's important that the leader gives everyone a chance to talk.

③例えば、リーダーは、ずっと黙っている人を見つけたら、その人に意見を述べるよう勧めるべきです。
For example, if the leader notices that one person is being quiet, she should invite that person to give an opinion.

❖ 練習しよう：❶ 単語ごとに英訳しよう
　　　　　　　❷「 / 」ごとに英訳しよう

B1 Could you tell me what kind of things the person in charge of a meeting should be careful about?

①私　思う　/その　リーダー　/その　人　に　責任　/の　1つの　会議
I think / the leader, / the person in charge / of a meeting,

/べき　わかりやすく　説明する　/その　目的　の　その　会議
/ should clearly explain / the purpose of the meeting

/そして　確かにする　/その　グループ　ままでいる　集中した。
/ and make sure / the group stays focused.

②私　また　思う　/それだ　重要　/ということ　その　リーダー
I also think / it's important / that the leader

/与える　すべての人　/1つの　チャンス　話すための。
/ gives everyone / a chance to talk.

③例えば　/もし　その　リーダー　気づく
For example, / if the leader notices

/ということ　1つの　人　だ　だ　静か
/ that one person is being quiet,

/彼　や　彼女　べき　招待する　その　人　与えること　1つの　意見。
/ he or she should invite that person / to give an opinion.

❖ 覚えよう

B1 **Could you tell me what kind of things the person in charge of a meeting should be careful about?**

I think the leader, the person in charge of a meeting, should clearly explain the purpose of the meeting and make sure the group stays focused. I also think it's important that the leader gives everyone a chance to talk. For example, if the leader notices that one person is being quiet, he or she should invite that person to give an opinion.

❖ 話してみよう

> **A1** Do you like participating in meetings?
>
> **A2** What advice would you give to a person who wants to give her opinion at a meeting but feels too shy to speak?
>
> **B1** If you were in charge of a conference on improving education in Japan, what kind of events would you plan?

88 The Human Body
人体

❖ 質問しよう

A1 あなたは今までに解剖学の授業をとったことがありますか。
Have you ever taken an anatomy class?

A2 いくつか主な器官の名前を教えてください。
Could you name some of the major organs?

B1 肺の機能について話してください。
Would you describe the function of the lungs?

❖ 答えよう

A1 Have you ever taken an anatomy class?
はい。// いいえ。// はい、あります。// いいえ、ありません。// 高校時代に。
Yes. // No. // Yes, I have. // No, I haven't. // In high school.

A2 Could you name some of the major organs?
いくつか名前を挙げると、心臓、肺、そして肝臓などです。
There is the heart, the lungs, and the liver to name a few.

B1 Would you describe the function of the lungs?
①肺の機能は2つあります。
The function of the lungs is twofold.

②まず、肺は空気から酸素を取り入れます。
First, the lungs obtain oxygen from the air.

③酸素が肺に入ると、その酸素は血流を通じて体全体に運ばれます。
When the oxygen is in the lungs, it is distributed via the bloodstream throughout the body.

④酸素は、その後、二酸化炭素と呼ばれるガスに変換され、血流を通じて肺に戻されます。

The oxygen is then exchanged for a gas called carbon dioxide, which is carried by the bloodstream back to the lungs.

⑤肺の2つ目の機能は、その後このガスを体から排出することです。

The second function of the lungs is then to exhale this gas out of the body.

❖ 練習しよう：❶ 単語ごとに英訳しよう
　　　　　　❷「／」ごとに英訳しよう

B1 **Would you describe the function of the lungs?**

①その　機能　の　その　肺　／だ　2部分。

The function of the lungs / is twofold.

②最初に　／その　肺　獲得する　酸素　／から　その　空気。

First, / the lungs obtain oxygen / from the air.

③時　その　酸素　だ　中に　その　肺

When the oxygen is in the lungs,

／それ　だ　運ばれる　／通して　その　血流　／隅から隅まで　その　体。

/ it is distributed / via the bloodstream / throughout the body.

④その　酸素　だ　それから　／交換される　ために　1つの　ガス

The oxygen is then / exchanged for a gas

／呼ばれる　二酸化炭素　／それ　だ　運ばれる　／によって　その血流

/ called carbon dioxide, / which is carried / by the bloodstream

／後ろ　に　その　肺。

/ back to the lungs.

⑤その　二番目　機能　／の　その　肺　だ

The second function / of the lungs is

／それから　／排出すること　この　ガス　／外へ　の　その　体。

/ then / to exhale this gas / out of the body.

❖ 覚えよう

B1 **Would you describe the function of the lungs?**

The function of the lungs is twofold. First, the lungs obtain oxygen from the air. When the oxygen is in the lungs, it is distributed via the bloodstream throughout the body. The oxygen is then exchanged for a gas called carbon dioxide, which is carried by the bloodstream back to the lungs. The second function of the lungs is then to exhale this gas out of the body.

❖ 話してみよう

A1 Do you ever read articles about how the human body works?

A2 Which is the most important of the five senses and why?

B1 What do elementary school students need to know about how the human body works?

89 Medical Treatment
医療

❖ 質問しよう

A1 あなたはよく病気になりますか。
Do you often get sick?

A2 あなたは風邪を引いたときにどうしますか。
What do you do when you catch a cold?

B1 風邪薬の副作用を説明してください。
Could you describe the side effects of cold medicine?

❖ 答えよう

A1 Do you often get sick?
はい。// いいえ。// はい、なります。// いいえ、なりません。// いいえ、そう多くはありません。
Yes. // No. // Yes, I do. // No, I don't. // No, not often.

A2 What do you do when you catch a cold?
私は熱いお茶を飲んでできるだけ睡眠をとります。温かい服も着ます。
I drink hot tea and sleep as much as I can. I wear warm clothes, too.

B1 Could you describe the side effects of cold medicine?
①考えられる副作用はたくさんあります。
There are many possible side effects.

②めまい、吐き気、ドライマウスなどがその典型です。
Some typical ones include dizziness, nausea, and dry mouth.

③最も一般的な副作用は、おそらく眠気です。だから、風邪薬を飲んだ後には運転すべきではないのです。
The most common side effect is probably drowsiness, which is why we shouldn't drive after taking cold medicine.

④長い期間にわたって、風邪薬を飲み続けると、肝臓を悪くすることもあります。

Taking certain cold medicines over a long period of time could result in liver damage.

❖ 練習しよう：❶ 単語ごとに英訳しよう
　　　　　　　❷「 / 」ごとに英訳しよう

B1 Could you describe the side effects of cold medicine?

①そこに　ある　/ 多くの　可能な　副作用。
There are / many possible side effects.

②いくつかの　典型的な　1つ　含む　/ めまい　/ 吐き気
Some typical ones include / dizziness, / nausea,

/ そして　ドライマウス。
/ and dry mouth.

③その　最も　一般的な　副作用　だ　/ おそらく　眠気
The most common side effect is / probably drowsiness,

/ それ　だ　なぜ　/ 私たち　べきでない　運転する
/ which is why / we shouldn't drive

/ 後　とること　風邪薬。
/ after taking cold medicine.

④とること　ある種の　風邪薬
Taking certain cold medicines

/ にわたって　1つの　長い　期間　の　時間
/ over a long period of time

/ できた　帰結する　/ に　肝臓　ダメージ。
/ could result / in liver damage.

❖ 覚えよう

B1 Could you describe the side effects of cold medicine?

There are many possible side effects. Some typical ones include dizziness, nausea, and dry mouth. The most common side effect is probably drowsiness, which is why we shouldn't drive after taking cold medicine. Taking certain cold medicines over a long period of time could result in liver damage.

❖ 話してみよう

> A1 Have you gone to see a doctor in the last month?
> A2 How does a person become a doctor in Japan?
> B1 In your opinion, how will medical treatment change in the next fifty years?

90 Health & Beauty
美容・健康

❖ 質問しよう

A1 あなたは美容製品に興味がありますか。
Are you interested in beauty products?

A2 健康を維持するために最も重要なことは何ですか。
What is the most important thing for you to stay healthy?

B1 最近人気のダイエット法について話してください。
Could you describe a recent popular diet?

❖ 答えよう

A1 Are you interested in beauty products?
はい。// いいえ。// はい、あります。// いいえ、ありません。// あまり。
Yes. // No. // Yes, I am. // No, I'm not. // Not really.

A2 What is the most important thing for you to stay healthy?
最も重要なことは水を飲むことだと思います。水は何よりも我々の体に必要なものです。
I think the most important thing is to drink water. We need water for our bodies more than anything else.

B1 Could you describe a recent popular diet?
①「レコーディング・ダイエット」が2、3年前にとてもはやりました。
The "recording diet" was pretty popular a few years ago.

②やり方は簡単です。
It's a simple idea.

③ただ食べるものすべてをリストにまとめます。
You just keep a list of everything that you eat.

④食べたもの、食べた量、そしていつ食べたかを記録します。
You write what you ate, how much you ate and when you ate it.

90 Health & Beauty 美容・健康

⑤たぶんこれによって食べるものに対する関心が高まって、このダイエットをしている多くの人たちは、何を食べるべきか、食べるべきでないかについて、より的確な判断ができるようになるのだと思います。

I think it helps you to become more conscious of what you eat, and because of this, many people on the diet use better judgment when deciding what to eat and what not to eat.

❖ 練習しよう：❶ 単語ごとに英訳しよう
　　　　　　❷「／」ごとに英訳しよう

B1 Could you describe a recent popular diet?

①その　レコーディング・ダイエット　／だった　かなり　人気がある
The "recording diet" / was pretty popular

／2、3年　前。
/ a few years ago.

②それだ　1つの　シンプルな　アイディア。
It's a simple idea.

③あなた　ただ　キープする　／1つの　リスト　の　すべて。
You just keep / a list of everything

／それ　あなた　食べる
/ that you eat.

④あなた　書く　／何　あなた　食べた　／どのくらい　あなた　食べた
You write / what you ate, / how much you ate

／そして　いつ　あなた　食べた　それ。
/ and when you ate it.

⑤私　思う　／それ　助ける　あなた　／なること　より　意識的
I think / it helps you / to become more conscious

／の　何　あなた　食べる　／そして　せいで　これ
/ of what you eat, / and because of this,

／多くの　人々　に　その　ダイエット　／使う　よりよい　判断
/ many people on the diet / use better judgment

/時　決めている　/何　食べること　/そして　何　ない　食べること。
/ when deciding / what to eat / and what not to eat.

❖ 覚えよう

B1 Could you describe a recent popular diet?

The "recording diet" was pretty popular a few years ago. It's a simple idea. You just keep a list of everything that you eat. You write what you ate, how much you ate and when you ate it. I think it helps you to become more conscious of what you eat, and because of this, many people on the diet use better judgment when deciding what to eat and what not to eat.

❖ 話してみよう

A1 Do you try to eat healthy food?
A2 Could you describe a healthy breakfast?
B1 Could you present a plan for a healthy lifestyle?

91 Animals
動物

❖ 質問しよう

> **A1** あなたは今までにペットを飼ったことがありますか。
> Have you ever had a pet?
>
> **A2** あなたの大好きな動物は何ですか。
> What is your favorite kind of animal?
>
> **B1** どのようにペットの世話をするか説明してください。
> Could you describe how to take care of a pet?

❖ 答えよう

A1 **Have you ever had a pet?**
はい。// いいえ。// はい、あります。// いいえ、ありません。
Yes. // No. // Yes, I have. // No, I haven't.

A2 **What is your favorite kind of animal?**
私は犬が一番好きです。猫が動物の中で一番好きな動物です。
I like dogs the best. // Cats are my favorite kind of animal.

B1 **Could you describe how to take care of a pet?**
①私は犬の世話について話します。

I'll talk about taking care of a dog.

②当然のことながら、すべての犬には食べ物が必要です。

Obviously, all dogs need food.

③ほとんどの犬は、1日に2回食べる必要があります。

Most dogs need to eat twice a day.

④犬たちには運動も必要ですが、ある犬種は他の犬種よりも多く運動を要求します。

They also need exercise, but some breeds require more than others.

⑤ほとんどの人が毎日きちんと犬と散歩し、多くの人が物を投げて犬に取って来させる遊びをします。

Most people walk their dogs regularly and many play fetch with them.

⑥獣医に連れて行って定期的に健診を受けさせ、犬の健康を維持することも重要なことです。

It's also important to maintain a dog's health by taking him to the veterinarian for regular checkups.

⑦もしこれらの基本的な欲求が満たされるのであれば、犬は幸せで健康な生活を送ることができるでしょう。

If these basic needs are met, a dog should have a happy and healthy life.

❖ 練習しよう：❶ 単語ごとに英訳しよう
❷「／」ごとに英訳しよう

B1 Could you describe how to take care of a pet?

①私だろう　話す　／について　世話をすること　／の　1つの　犬。
I'll talk / about taking care / of a dog.

②明らかに　／すべての　犬　必要とする　食べ物。
Obviously, / all dogs need food.

③ほとんどの　犬　必要とする　／食べること　2回　1つの　日。
Most dogs need / to eat twice a day.

④彼ら　また　必要とする　運動
They also need exercise,

／しかし　／いくつかの　犬種　要求する　／より多く　よりも　他。
/ but / some breeds require / more than others.

⑤ほとんどの　人　／歩かせる　彼らの　犬　規則正しく　／そして
Most people / walk their dogs regularly / and

／多く　投げた物を取って来させる遊びをする　／と一緒に　彼ら。
/ many play fetch / with them.

⑥それだ　また　重要　／維持すること　1つの　犬の　健康
It's also important / to maintain a dog's health

/によって 連れて行くこと 彼 /に その 獣医
/ by taking him / to the veterinarian

/のために 定期的な 健診。
/ for regular checkups.

⑦もし /これらの 基本的な ニーズ だ 満たされる
If / these basic needs are met,

/1つの 犬 べき 持つ
/ a dog should have

/1つの ハッピーな そして 健康な 生活。
/ a happy and healthy life.

❖ 覚えよう

B1 Could you describe how to take care of a pet?

I'll talk about taking care of a dog. Obviously, all dogs need food. Most dogs need to eat twice a day. They also need exercise, but some breeds require more than others. Most people walk their dogs regularly and many play fetch with them. It's also important to maintain a dog's health by taking him to the veterinarian for regular checkups. If these basic needs are met, a dog should have a happy and healthy life.

❖ 話してみよう

A1 Do you prefer dogs or cats?
A2 What kind of animal makes the best pet and why?
B1 Could you describe an animal that has an interesting or unique quality?

92 Plants
植物

❖ 質問しよう

> **A1** あなたは今までに植物を育てたことがありますか。
> Have you ever grown a plant?
>
> **A2** あなたの大好きな花は何ですか。
> What is your favorite kind of flower?
>
> **B1** 自宅に植物を置く利点をいくつか挙げてください。
> What are some of the benefits of having plants in your home?

❖ 答えよう

A1 Have you ever grown a plant?

はい。// いいえ。// はい、あります。// いいえ、ありません。// もちろん。

Yes. // No. // Yes, I have. // No, I haven't. // Sure.

A2 What is your favorite kind of flower?

私の大好きな花は紫陽花です。// 私はその青色が好きです。

I think my favorite flower is hydrangea. I like the blue color.

B1 What are some of the benefits of having plants in your home?

①利点は3つあると思います。

I can think of three reasons.

②まず、植物が部屋にあると、ない部屋と比較してはるかに安らぎを感じるし、リラックスできます。

First, I've always thought that a room with plants feels much more comfortable and relaxing than a room without them.

③2つめに、植物は酸素を作るので、植物を置くことで人により健康的な環境を作ることができます。
Second, plants produce oxygen, so I think having plants creates a healthier environment for people.

④3つめに、自宅にミントやバジルなど食べられる植物を植えることはとてもよいと思います。
Third, it can be nice to keep edible plants like mint or basil in your home.

⑤新鮮なハーブを摘み料理に使えればとても楽しいですね。
It's fun to pick fresh herbs and use them when you're cooking.

❖ 練習しよう：❶ 単語ごとに英訳しよう
　　　　　　❷「/」ごとに英訳しよう

B1 What are some of the benefits of having plants in your home?

①私　できる　思う　/の　3つの　理由。
I can think / of three reasons.

②最初に　/私持つ　いつも　思った
First, / I've always thought

/ということ　1つの　部屋　と一緒に　植物
/ that a room with plants

/感じる　ずっと　よりも　心地よい　/そして　リラックスできる
/ feels much more comfortable / and relaxing

/よりも　1つの　部屋　/〜なしの　それら。
/ than a room / without them.

③2番めに　/植物　製造する　酸素　/だから　/私　思う
Second, / plants produce oxygen, / so / I think

/持つこと　植物　創造する　/1つの　より健康的な　環境
/ having plants creates / a healthier environment

/のために　人々。
/ for people.

276

④3番めに / それ できる だ 素敵
Third, / it can be nice

/ キープすること 食べられる 植物
/ to keep edible plants

/ のような ミント または バジル / に あなたの 家。
/ like mint or basil / in your home.

⑤それだ 楽しい / 摘むこと 新鮮な ハーブ / そして 使う それら
It's fun / to pick fresh herbs / and use them

/ 時 あなただ 料理している。
/ when you're cooking.

❖ 覚えよう

B1 **What are some of the benefits of having plants in your home?**

I can think of three reasons. First, I've always thought that a room with plants feels much more comfortable and relaxing than a room without them. Second, plants produce oxygen, so I think having plants creates a healthier environment for people. Third, it can be nice to keep edible plants like mint or basil in your home. It's fun to pick fresh herbs and use them when you're cooking.

❖ 話してみよう

A1 Do you think plants have feelings?

A2 Why are some people successful at growing plants while others are not?

B1 Could you describe the process of growing a flower from a seed?

93 Weather
気象

❖ 質問しよう

A1 あなたは普段テレビで天気予報を見ますか。
Do you regularly watch the weather forecast on TV?

A2 なぜあなたはテレビで天気予報を見る／見ないのですか。
Why do/don't you watch weather forecast on TV?

B1 テレビの予報を見ずに天気を予測する方法をいくつか教えてください。
Could you tell me some ways to predict the weather without watching the forecast on TV?

❖ 答えよう

A1 Do you regularly watch the weather forecast on TV?
はい。// いいえ。// はい、見ます。// いいえ、見ません。// 時々。
Yes. // No. // Yes, I do. // No, I don't. // Sometimes.

A2 Why do/don't you watch weather forecast on TV?
私は天気はいつも携帯でチェックするので、テレビの天気予報は見ません。
I don't watch the weather forecast on TV because I always check the weather on my phone.

B1 Could you tell me some ways to predict the weather without watching the forecast on TV?

①私はいつも空をチェックします。
I always check the sky.

②もし黒い雲があったら、雨が降るかもしれないとわかります。
If I see dark clouds, I know it might rain.

③もし晴れていて、風がなければ、天気はたぶんよくなるだろうということがわかります。
If there are clear skies and no wind, I know the weather will probably be good.

④もし風が強ければ、天気が変わることがわかります。
If it's really windy, I know that the weather may change.

⑤また、夜に月のまわりに輪ができていたら、まもなく雨か雪が降るだろうということを聞いたことがあります。
I've also heard that if you see a ring around the moon at night, it will probably rain or snow soon.

❖ 練習しよう：❶ 単語ごとに英訳しよう
　　　　　　　❷「／」ごとに英訳しよう

B1 Could you tell me some ways to predict the weather without watching the forecast on TV?

①私　いつも　チェックする　／その　空。
I always check / the sky.

②もし　私　見る　暗い　雲　／私　知る
If I see dark clouds, / I know

／それ　かもしれなかった　雨が降る。
/ it might rain.

③もし　そこに　ある　晴れた　空　／そして　ない　風
If there are clear skies / and no wind,

／私　知る　／その　天気　だろう　おそらく　／だ　よい。
/ I know / the weather will probably / be good.

④もし　それだ　本当に　風が強い
If it's really windy,

／私　知る　／ということ　その　天候　かもしれない　変わる。
/ I know / that the weather may change.

⑤私持つ　また　聞いた　ということ　／もし　あなた　見る　１つの　輪
I've also heard that / if you see a ring

/ のまわり その 月 / に 夜 / それ だろう おそらく 雨が降る
/ around the moon / at night, / it will probably rain

/ または 雪が降る まもなく。
/ or snow soon.

❖ 覚えよう

B1 **Could you tell me some ways to predict the weather without watching the forecast on TV?**

I always check the sky. If I see dark clouds, I know it might rain. If there are clear skies and no wind, I know the weather will probably be good. If it's really windy, I know that the weather may change. I've also heard that if you see a ring around the moon at night, it will probably rain or snow soon.

❖ 話してみよう

A1 Do you like rainy days?

A2 What is your favorite kind of weather?

B1 Why does weather affect people's moods?

94 Nature & Geographical Features
自然・地勢

❖ 質問しよう

A1 日本には地形に珍しい特徴を持つ観光地はありますか。

Is there a sightseeing spot with unusual land features in Japan?

A2 日本のどの地形が最も珍しいと思いますか。

Which land features in Japan are most unusual?

B1 火山活動が日本列島にどんな影響を与えているか説明してください。

Could you explain how volcanic activity affects the Japanese islands?

❖ 答えよう

A1 **Is there a sightseeing spot with unusual land features in Japan?**

はい。// いいえ。// いいえ、思いつきません。

Yes. // No. // Not that I can think of.

A2 **Which land features in Japan are most unusual?**

素晴らしい海岸段丘が見られる三陸海岸が日本で最も地形に珍しい特徴を持つ場所だと思います。

I think the area called Sanriku Coast, where you can see amazing coastal terraces, is the most unusual land feature in Japan.

B1 **Could you explain how volcanic activity affects the Japanese islands?**

①火山活動は日本列島に非常に大きな影響を与えています。

Volcanic activity greatly affects the Japanese islands.

94　Nature & Geographical Features　自然・地勢

②日本には環太平洋火山帯に所属する 100 を超える活火山があります。
Japan is home to over a hundred active volcanoes, which belong to the Pacific Ring of Fire.

③時折起きる噴火によって、破片、煙そして灰が空に舞い上がり、飛行機が被害のある地域を避けて飛行することはもちろんのこと、住民は最もひどく被害を受ける地域から避難を余儀なくされます。
Occasional eruptions occur which send debris, smoke and ash flying into the sky, forcing the inhabitants to evacuate the hardest hit areas, as well as diverting airplanes from flying over the affected areas.

❖ 練習しよう：❶ 単語ごとに英訳しよう
　　　　　　　　❷「 / 」ごとに英訳しよう

B1 Could you explain how volcanic activity affects the Japanese islands?

①火山の　活動は　/ 多大に　影響する　/ その　日本の　島。
Volcanic activity / greatly affects / the Japanese islands.

②日本　だ　家 /に　超える　1つの　100　活動的な　火山
Japan is home / to over a hundred active volcanoes,

/ それ　所属する / に　その　環太平洋火山帯。
/ which belong / to the Pacific Ring of Fire.

③時々の　噴火　起こる / それ　送る　破片 / 煙 / そして　灰
Occasional eruptions occur / which send debris, / smoke / and ash

/ 飛んでいく　の中に　その　空 / 強制しながら　その　住人
/ flying into the sky, / forcing the inhabitants

/ 避難すること　その　一番ハードに　打たれた　エリア
/ to evacuate the hardest hit areas,

/ と同様に　そらすこと　飛行機 / から　飛ぶこと
/ as well as diverting airplanes / from flying

/ の上を　その　影響された　エリア。
/ over the affected areas.

❖ 覚えよう

B1 **Could you explain how volcanic activity affects the Japanese islands?**

Volcanic activity greatly affects the Japanese islands. Japan is home to over a hundred active volcanoes, which belong to the Pacific Ring of Fire. Occasional eruptions occur, which send debris, smoke and ash flying into the sky, forcing the inhabitants to evacuate the hardest hit areas, as well as diverting airplanes from flying over the affected areas.

❖ 話してみよう

A1 Do you think Mt. Fuji is beautiful?

A2 In your opinion, what is the most interesting kind of landscape?

B1 How has being an island nation affected Japanese culture?

95 Disaster
災害

❖ 質問しよう

A1 あなたは今までに大きな地震を経験したことがありますか。
Have you ever experienced a big earthquake?

A2 あなたが最後に地震を経験したのはいつですか。
When was the last time you experienced an earthquake?

B1 大地震が起きたらどうすべきかを教えてください。
Could you tell me what we should do when there is a big earthquake?

❖ 答えよう

A1 Have you ever experienced a big earthquake?
はい。// いいえ。// はい、あります。// いいえ、ありません。
Yes. // No. // Yes, I have. // No, I haven't.

A2 When was the last time you experienced an earthquake?
昨日実際に地震がありました。
There was actually one yesterday.

B1 Could you tell me what we should do when there is a big earthquake?

①一般的に言って、最初にすべきことは落ち着くことです。パニックになってはいけません。
Generally speaking, the first thing you should do is to stay calm—don't panic.

②落下物から身を守ることが重要で、テーブルの下に入るかあるいは枕で頭を覆います。
It is important to protect yourself from falling objects so you should get under a table or cover your head with a pillow.

③もちろん、コンロの火や、火災の原因になりそうな他のものを消すことも必要です。

Of course, you should also turn off the stove and anything else that could cause a fire.

④揺れが止まったら、事前に指定された地域に避難する必要があるかもしれません。

After the shaking stops, you may need to evacuate to a pre-designated area.

❖ 練習しよう：❶ 単語ごとに英訳しよう
　　　　　　　❷「／」ごとに英訳しよう

B1 Could you tell me what we should do when there is a big earthquake?

①一般的に言って ／その　最初の　こと ／あなた　べき　する
Generally speaking, / the first thing / you should do

／だ　ままでいること　落ち着いている ／ない　パニックになる。
/ is to stay calm / —don't panic.

②それ　だ　重要 ／守ること　あなた自身 ／から　落下している　物体
It is important / to protect yourself / from falling objects

／だから ／あなた　べき　得る ／の下に　1つの　テーブル
/ so / you should get / under a table

／または　カバーする　あなたの　頭 ／と一緒に　1つの　枕。
/ or cover your head / with a pillow.

③もちろん ／あなた　べき　また ／消す　その　コンロ
Of course, / you should also / turn off the stove

／そして　何か　他に ／それ　できた　起こす ／1つの　火災。
/ and anything else / that could cause / a fire.

④の後で　その　揺れること　止まる
After the shaking stops,

／あなた　かもしれない　必要だ　避難すること
/ you may need to evacuate

/に 1つの 事前に指定された エリア。
/ to a pre-designated area.

❖ 覚えよう

B1 Could you tell me what we should do when there is a big earthquake?

Generally speaking, the first thing you should do is to stay calm—don't panic. It is important to protect yourself from falling objects so you should get under a table or cover your head with a pillow. Of course, you should also turn off the stove and anything else that could cause a fire. After the shaking stops, you may need to evacuate to a pre-designated area.

❖ 話してみよう

> **A1** When you were in elementary school, did you have emergency drills?
>
> **A2** How have you prepared for an emergency at your home?
>
> **B1** What is the most dangerous kind of natural disaster and why?

96 The Earth's Environment
環境問題

❖ 質問しよう

> **A1** あなたは環境に優しい生活をしていますか。
> Do you have an eco-friendly lifestyle?
>
> **A2** 環境に優しい習慣をいくつか挙げてください。
> What are some common eco-friendly habits?
>
> **B1** 日常生活でより環境に優しい生活をするためにはどうすべきですか。
> How can you become more eco-friendly in your daily life?

❖ 答えよう

A1 **Do you have an eco-friendly lifestyle?**
はい。// いいえ。// はい、しています。// いいえ、していません。// していると思います。// たぶんしていません。

Yes. // No. // Yes, I do. // No, I don't. // I think so. // Maybe not.

A2 **What are some common eco-friendly habits?**
車を使う代わりに自転車に乗ったり歩いたりすることは、環境に優しくする1つの方法です。

Riding a bicycle or walking instead of using a car is one way to be more eco-friendly.

B1 **How can you become more eco-friendly in your daily life?**
①えーと、たくさんのことができると思います。

Well, I suppose I could do many things.

②常にエコバックを持ち歩けばビニール袋を使う必要がなくなります。

I could carry an eco-bag around all the time so I wouldn't have to use plastic bags.

③プラスチックの容器をたくさん使った製品を買うことをやめることもできます。
I could stop buying products that have a lot of plastic packaging.

④エアコンをできるだけ使わないようにすることもできます。
I could use the air conditioner less.

⑤ソーラーパネルを設置することさえできます。
I could even have solar panels installed.

⑥小規模なものから大規模なものまで、できることはたくさんあります。
There are lots of things I can do—some small and some big.

❖ 練習しよう：❶ 単語ごとに英訳しよう
　　　　　　　❷「／」ごとに英訳しよう

B1 How can you become more eco-friendly in your daily life?

①えー ／私 仮定する ／私 できた する ／多くの こと。
Well, / I suppose / I could do / many things.

②私 できた 運ぶ 1つの エコバック まわりに
I could carry an eco-bag around

／すべての その 時間 ／だから
/ all the time / so

／私 ないだろう なければならない 使う ／プラスチック バッグ。
/ I wouldn't have to use / plastic bags.

③私 できた やめる ／買うこと 製品
I could stop / buying products

／それ 持つ たくさんの プラスチック パッケージ。
/ that have a lot of plastic packaging.

④私は できた 使う ／その エアコン ／より少なく。
I could use / the air conditioner / less.

⑤私は できた さえ ／持つ ソーラーパネル 設置される。
I could even / have solar panels installed.

⑥そこに　ある　たくさんの　もの　/私　できる　する
There are lots of things / I can do

/いくつか　小さい　/そして　いくつか　大きい。
/ —some small / and some big.

❖ 覚えよう

B1 **How can you become more eco-friendly in your daily life?**

Well, I suppose I could do many things. I could carry an eco-bag around all the time so I wouldn't have to use plastic bags. I could stop buying products that have a lot of plastic packaging. I could use the air conditioner less. I could even have solar panels installed. There are lots of things I can do—some small and some big.

❖ 話してみよう

A1 Do you think the environment is in danger?

A2 What are some of the threats to the environment?

B1 How have businesses benefited from using the term eco?

97 Space
宇宙

❖ 質問しよう

> **A1** あなたは今までに天体望遠鏡を使ったことがありますか。
> Have you ever used a telescope?
>
> **A2** 英語でいくつかの惑星の名前を言ってください。
> Can you name some of the planets in English?
>
> **B1** なぜ日食・月食が起きるのか説明してください。
> Could you explain why eclipses occur?

❖ 答えよう

A1 Have you ever used a telescope?

はい。// いいえ。// はい、あります。// いいえ、ありません。// 一度。// 一度も。

Yes. // No. // Yes, I have. // No, I haven't // Once. // Never.

A2 Can you name some of the planets in English?

そうですね、水星、金星そして地球から始まって8つありますね。

Let's see… there are eight, starting with Mercury, Venus, and Earth.

B1 Could you explain why eclipses occur?

①基本的には、日食と月食があります。

Basically, there are solar eclipses and lunar eclipses.

②日食は、月が地球と太陽の間を通る時に起きます。

A solar eclipse occurs when the moon passes between the earth and the sun.

③部分日食は月が太陽の一部分をふさぐ時に起きます。そして、皆既日食は、月が太陽をすっぽり覆ってしまう時に起きます。

There are partial solar eclipses, when the moon blocks part of the sun, and total eclipses, when the moon blocks all of the sun.

④月食は、月が地球の影の中を通る時に起きます。

Lunar eclipses occur when the moon passes into the earth's shadow.

⑤これが起きるためには、地球は太陽と月の間にいなければいけません。

For this to happen, the earth must be between the sun and moon.

⑥時間を作って、日食・月食を観察する人は多いです。

Many people make time to observe eclipses.

❖ 練習しよう：❶ 単語ごとに英訳しよう
　　　　　　 ❷「／」ごとに英訳しよう

B1 Could you explain why eclipses occur?

①基本的に ／そこに ある 日食 ／そして 月食。

Basically, / there are solar eclipses / and lunar eclipses.

②1つの 日食 起きる ／時 その 月 過ぎる

A solar eclipse occurs / when the moon passes

／の間 その 地球 そして その 太陽。

/ between the earth and the sun.

③そこに ある 部分的な 日食 ／時 その 月 ブロックする

There are partial eclipses, / when the moon blocks

／部分 の その 太陽 ／そして 皆既日食

/ part of the sun, / and total eclipses,

／時 その 月 ブロックする ／すべて の その 太陽。

/ when the moon blocks / all of the sun.

④月食 起きる ／時 その 月 過ぎる

Lunar eclipses occur / when the moon passes

／の中に その 地球の 影。

/ into the earth's shadow.

⑤のため これ ため 起こる ／その 地球 なければならない だ

For this to happen, / the earth must be

の間　その　太陽　そして　月。
/ between the sun and moon.

⑥多くの　人々　作る　時間　/ ために　観察する　食。
Many people make time / to observe eclipses.

❖ 覚えよう

B1 **Could you explain why eclipses occur?**

Basically, there are solar eclipses and lunar eclipses. A solar eclipse occurs when the moon passes between the earth and the sun. There are partial solar eclipses, when the moon blocks part of the sun, and total eclipses, when the moon blocks all of the sun. Lunar eclipses occur when the moon passes into the earth's shadow. For this to happen, the earth must be between the sun and moon. Many people make time to observe eclipses.

❖ 話してみよう

> **A1** Do you like to look at the stars?
> **A2** In addition to stars and planets, what other things are found in space?
> **B1** What is your opinion about the possibility of life on other planets?

98 Mathematics
算数・数学

❖ 質問しよう

> **A1** 2足す2はいくつですか。
> What is two plus two?
>
> **A2** あなたが数学を勉強し始めたのはいつですか。
> When did you start learning math?
>
> **B1** 日々の生活で数学を使う一般的な方法を1つ述べてください。
> Could you explain a common way to use math in everyday life?

❖ 答えよう

A1 What is two plus two?

4です。

Four.

A2 When did you start learning math?

3歳の時に数学を学び始めたと思います。幼稚園で習いました。

I think I started learning math when I was three. I learned it in preschool.

B1 Could you explain a common way to use math in everyday life?

①標準的な紙のサイズは、数学の公式に基づいています。

Standard paper sizes are based on a mathematical formula.

②例えば、A4用紙はA3用紙のちょうど半分のサイズで、両者は相似形です。

Foe example, A4 paper is exactly half the size of A3 paper, and they are similar figures.

③A3の紙の縦と横の長さXとYとすれば、A4の紙の縦と横はYとX/2になります。
If you suppose the length and width of a sheet of A3 paper to be X and Y, those of a sheet of A4 paper become Y and X/2 (X divided by 2).

④内項の積は外項の積に等しいという性質から、Y×Y＝X×X/2という式が得られます。
According to the means-extremes property of proportions, you get the formula: Y*Y=X*X/2 (Y times Y equals X times X divided by 2).

⑤この方程式を解くと、X：Y＝√2：1となります。
By solving this equation, you can find X : Y=√2 : 1(X to Y equals the square root of 2 to 1).

❖ 練習しよう：❶ 単語ごとに英訳しよう
　　　　　　❷「／」ごとに英訳しよう

B1 Could you explain a common way to use math in everyday life?

①標準的な　紙　サイズ　/だ　基づいた　/に　1つの　数学の　公式。
Standard paper sizes / are based / on a mathematical formula.

②例えば /A4　紙　だ　正確に　半分　その　サイズ　/の　A3　紙
Foe example, /A4 paper is exactly half the size / of A3 paper,

/そして　それら　だ　相似形。
/ and they are similar figures.

③もし　あなた　仮定する　/その　縦　と　横
If you suppose / the length and width

/の　1つの　シート　の　A3　紙　/であること　X　と　Y
/ of a sheet of A3 paper / to be X and Y,

/それら　の　1つの　シート　の　A4　紙　なる
/ those of a sheet of A4 paper become

/Y　と　X　分けられる　によって　2。
/ Y and X/2 (X divided by 2).

④よると に 内向の積は外向の積に等しいという性質
According to the means-extremes property of proportions,

/あなた 得る その 式
/ you get the formula:

/Y かける Y 等しい X かける X 分けられる によって 2。
/ Y*Y=X*X/2 (Y times Y equals X times X divided by 2).

⑤によって 解くこと この 方程式 /あなた できる 得る
By solving this equation, / you can find

/X に Y 等しい その スクエアルート の 2 に 1。
/ X : Y=√2 : 1 (X to Y equals the square root of 2 to 1).

❖ 覚えよう

B1 **Could you explain a common way to use math in everyday life?**

Standard paper sizes are based on a mathematical formula. For example, A4 paper is exactly half the size of A3 paper, and they are similar figures. If you suppose the length and width of a sheet of A3 paper to be X and Y, those of a sheet of A4 paper become Y and X/2 (X divided by 2). According to the means-extremes property of proportions, you get the formula: Y*Y=X*X/2 (Y times Y equals X times X divided by 2). By solving this equation, you can find X : Y=√2 : 1 (X to Y equals the square root of 2 to 1).

❖ 話してみよう

> **A1** Did you like math class when you were in high school?
>
> **A2** What is necessary to be a successful math teacher?
>
> **B1** What would you like to change about the way math is taught in school?

99 Science
サイエンス

❖ 質問しよう

> **A1** サメには体内に骨がありますか。
> Do sharks have bones in their bodies?
>
> **A2** 地球上でもっとも硬い物質は何ですか。
> What is the hardest substance on earth?
>
> **B1** 進化論を説明してください。
> Could you describe the theory of evolution?

❖ 答えよう

A1 **Do sharks have bones in their bodies?**
いいえ。// いいえ、ありません。// ないと思います。// わかりません。
No. // No, they don't. // I don't think so. // I don't know.

A2 **What is the hardest substance on earth?**
たぶん地球上で最も硬い物質はダイヤモンドだと思います。ダイヤモンドはとても硬いものを切る際に使われます。

I think the hardest substance on earth is a diamond. Diamonds are used to cut other things that are very hard.

B1 **Could you describe the theory of evolution?**
①進化論は、環境の変化による自然淘汰と呼ばれるプロセスを、生物が経ていくことを述べることによって説明できます。

The theory of evolution can be explained by saying that living things go through a process called natural selection due to changes in their environment.

②この淘汰のプロセスは、種の存続に役立つ場合にのみ保たれ続ける生物学的特徴において、見ることができます。

This selection process can be seen in certain biological traits that persist only as long as they help a species to survive.

③例えば、大昔、馬は森で生活していました。

A long time ago, for example, horses lived in forests.

④そのころ、馬は、その環境で生き残るために、より小さくある必要がありました。

At that time, they had to be much smaller to survive in their environment.

⑤しかし、やがて森は小さくなり、より大きな馬が平地で生き残る一方、小さな馬は消えていきました。

However, these forests eventually decreased in size, and small horses disappeared while bigger horses survived on the open land.

❖ 練習しよう：❶ 単語ごとに英訳しよう
　　　　　　　❷「/」ごとに英訳しよう

B1 Could you describe the theory of evolution?

①その　進化論　/できる　だ　説明される　/によって　言うこと

The theory of evolution / can be explained / by saying

/ということ　生きている　もの　通り抜ける　/1つの　プロセス

/ that living things go through / a process

/呼ばれる　自然淘汰　/のため　変化　/に　それらの　環境。

/ called natural selection / due to changes / in their environment.

②この　淘汰　プロセス　/できる　だ　見られる

This selection process / can be seen

/に　ある　生物学的な　特徴　/それ　存続する

/ in certain biological traits / that persist

/のみ　〜限り　/それら　助ける　1つの　種　/生き残ること。

/ only as long as / they help a species / to survive.

③大昔　/例えば　/馬　生活した　/に　森。

A long time ago, / for example, / horses lived / in forests.

④に　あの　時　/彼ら　なければならなかった　だ　ずっと　より小さい

At that time, / they had to be much smaller

/ために 生き残る /に 彼らの 環境。
/ to survive / in their environment.

⑤しかしながら /これらの 森 /やがて 減少した /において サイズ
However, / these forests / eventually decreased / in size,

/そして 小さい 馬 消えた /一方 より大きい 馬 生き残った
/ and small horses disappeared / while bigger horses survived

/上に その オープンな 土地。
/ on the open land.

❖ 覚えよう

B1 **Could you describe the theory of evolution?**

The theory of evolution can be explained by saying that living things go through a process called natural selection due to changes in their environment. This selection process can be seen in certain biological traits that persist only as long as they help a species to survive. A long time ago, for example, horses lived in forests. At that time, they had to be much smaller to survive in their environment. However, these forests eventually decreased in size, and small horses disappeared while bigger horses survived on the open land.

❖ 話してみよう

> **A1** Are you interested in science?
> **A2** What kind of science is most interesting to you?
> **B1** What is the most important scientific discovery and why?

100 Technology
テクノロジー

❖ 質問しよう

A1 あなたは今までに 3D のテレビ番組を観たことがありますか。
Have you ever watched a 3D TV program?

A2 あなたの携帯電話でメッセージを送る方法を説明してください。
Could you describe how to send a message on your phone?

B1 GPS について何か教えてください。
Could you tell us a little about GPS?

❖ 答えよう

A1 Have you ever watched a 3D TV program?
はい。// いいえ。// はい、あります。// たぶんないと思います。
Yes. // No. // Yes, I have. // I don't think so.

A2 Could you describe how to send a message on your phone?
はい、メッセージを書いて送信ボタンを押すだけです。簡単です。
Yes, just type your message and push the send button. It's easy.

B1 Could you tell us a little about GPS?
① GPS とは、Global Positioning System の略称です。
GPS stands for Global Positioning System.

② GPS のナビゲーション装置を使うことによって、世界中のどこにいても、自分がいる場所を知ることができます。
By using a GPS navigation device, we can determine our location anywhere in the world.

③ そのためには、装置が衛星からのシグナルを受け取る必要があります。
To do so, a device needs to receive signals from satellites.

④もともと、GPS は、アメリカ軍によって、アメリカ軍のために開発され、そして、その使用は制限されていました。
Originally it was developed by and for the US military, and its use was restricted.

⑤しかし、今日では、GPS は誰でも利用でき、ほとんどの人が GPS のことを深く考えることなく、それを使っています。
Nowadays, however, GPS is available to anybody, and most people use it without giving it much thought.

⑥しかし、実際、手に収まるサイズの装置が、何千キロも離れた空の上からの衛星のシグナルを受け取っているというのは、驚きです。
But actually, it's amazing that a handheld device can receive signals from satellites thousands of kilometers up in the sky.

❖ 練習しよう：❶ 単語ごとに英訳しよう　❷「 / 」ごとに英訳しよう

B1 Could you tell us a little about GPS?

① GPS　表す　/ Global Positioning System。
GPS stands for / Global Positioning System.

②によって　使うこと　/1つの　GPS　ナビゲーション　装置
By using / a GPS navigation device,

/ 私たち　できる　決める　/ 私たちの　居場所
/ we can determine / our location

/ どこでも　に　その　世界。
/ anywhere in the world.

③ために　する　そう　/1つの　装置　必要とする　受け取ること
To do so, / a device needs to receive

/ シグナル　から　衛星。
/ signals from satellites.

④もともと　/ それ　だった　開発される　/ によって　そして　のために
Originally / it was developed / by and for

/ その　合衆国　軍隊　/ そして　それの　使用　だった　制限される。
/ the US military, / and its use was restricted.

⑤今日では / しかしながら /GPS だ 利用可能 / に 誰でも
Nowadays, / however, / GPS is available / to anybody,

/ そして ほとんどの 人 使う それ
/ and most people use it

/ 〜なしに 与えること それ 多くの 考え。
/ without / giving it much thought.

⑥しかし 実際 / それだ 驚くこと
But actually, / it's amazing

/ ということ 1つの 手に収まる 装置 できる 受け取る
/ that a handheld device can receive

/ シグナル から 衛星 /数千 の キロメートル / 上 に その 空。
/ signals from satellites / thousands of kilometers / up in the sky.

❖ 覚えよう

B1 **Could you tell us a little about GPS?**

GPS stands for Global Positioning System. By using a GPS navigation device, we can determine our location anywhere in the world. To do so, a device needs to receive signals from satellites. Originally it was developed by and for the US military, and its use was restricted. Nowadays, however, GPS is available to anybody, and most people use it without giving it much thought. But actually, it's amazing that a handheld device can receive signals from satellites thousands of kilometers up in the sky.

❖ 話してみよう

A1 Do you like to read articles about technology?

A2 What is the most important technology in your life?

B1 What are some of the drawbacks of human dependence on technology?

著者略歴

中山誠一(なかやま・ともかず)
実践女子大学言語文化教育研究センター教授
著書に*Efficacy of Visual-Auditory Shadowing Method in SLA Based on Language Processing Models in Cognitive Psychology*, Kaitakusha, 2017.などがある。

Jacob Schnickel(ジェイコブ・シュニッケル)
実践女子大学言語文化教育研究センター准教授
論文に"Peer Coaching as Preparation for Study Abroad among Japanese University Students," *Journal of the College of Intercultural Communication, Vol. 3, Language, Culture, and Communication*, 209-223, 2011.などがある。

Juergen Bulach(ヨーガン・ブラック)
実践女子大学言語文化教育研究センター教授
論文に"A Case Study of Third-Language Acquistion: Analyzing the Transition from Bilingualism to Trilingualism," *Jissen Women's University FLC Journal, Vol. 6*, 35-42, 2011. などがある。

山内博之(やまうち・ひろゆき)
実践女子大学文学部国文学科教授
著書に『実践日本語教育スタンダード』(共著、ひつじ書房、2013年)などがある。

脱文法　100トピック実践英語トレーニング
Intuitive Grammar English Training: 100 Topics

Tomokazu Nakayama, Jacob Schnickel, Juergen Bulach, Hiroyuki Yamauchi

発行	2017年5月17日　初版1刷
	2024年4月18日　　　　5刷
定価	1600円＋税
著者	©中山誠一・Jacob Schnickel・Juergen Bulach・山内博之
発行者	松本功
装丁者	坂田由麻（asahi edigraphy）
本文組版者	上田かの子（asahi edigraphy）
印刷・製本所	三美印刷株式会社
発行所	株式会社 ひつじ書房
	〒112-0011 東京都文京区千石2-1-2　大和ビル2階
	Tel.03-5319-4916　Fax.03-5319-4917
	郵便振替00120-8-142852
	toiawase@hituzi.co.jp　https://www.hituzi.co.jp/

ISBN978-4-89476-858-1

造本には充分注意しておりますが、落丁・乱丁などがございましたら、小社かお買上げ書店にておとりかえいたします。ご意見、ご感想など、小社までお寄せ下されば幸いです。

[刊行書籍のご案内]

英語の学び方

大津由紀雄・嶋田珠巳編　　定価 1,500 円＋税

英語が使えるようになりたいと思っている人は多いが、悩みを抱える人もまた多い。本書では、英語学習を効果的かつ効率的に進めるために必要なことを、わかりやすく解説。英語の構造や機能、辞書の利用法のほか、類書ではあまり触れられることのない世界の諸英語やノンバーバル・コミュニケーションの視点も取り入れ、英語を学ぶ秘訣に迫る。

執筆者：大津由紀雄、瀧田健介、高田智子、津留崎毅、小林裕子、嶋田珠巳、原和也、遊佐昇、安井利一